STATE
COURT
SYSTEMS

HENRY ROBERT GLICK / KENNETH N. VINES

FOUNDATIONS
OF STATE
AND LOCAL
GOVERNMENT
SERIES

WALLACE S. SAYRE
Editor

STATE COURT SYSTEMS

FOUNDATIONS OF STATE AND LOCAL GOVERNMENT SERIES

WALLACE S. SAYRE, EDITOR

STATE LEGISLATIVE SYSTEMS
Wilder Crane, Jr. and *Meredith W. Watts, Jr.*

STATE COURT SYSTEMS
Henry Robert Glick and *Kenneth N. Vines*

HENRY ROBERT GLICK
Florida State University

KENNETH N. VINES
State University of New York at Buffalo

STATE

COURT

SYSTEMS

Prentice-Hall, Inc., Englewood Cliffs, New Jersey

Library of Congress Cataloging in Publication Data

GLICK, HENRY ROBERT.
    State court systems

([Foundations of state and local government series])
    Includes bibliographical references.
    1. Courts—United States—States. 2. Judges—United States—States.
    I. Vines, Kenneth Nelson.
        joint author. II. Title.
    KF8736.G54   347'.73'1   72-5742
    ISBN 0-13-842997-9

PRENTICE-HALL INTERNATIONAL, INC. *London*
PRENTICE-HALL OF AUSTRALIA, PTY. LTD. *Sydney*
PRENTICE-HALL OF CANADA, LTD. *Toronto*
PRENTICE-HALL OF INDIA PRIVATE LIMITED. *New Delhi*
PRENTICE-HALL OF JAPAN, INC. *Tokyo*

10   9   8   7   6   5   4   3   2   1

To Doris, Norma, and Mae—
the women in our lives
who have helped more than they know

CONTENTS

PREFACE

During the several years of the development of this work, we received help from many sources. Various grants from the Tulane Graduate Research Council, the Research Foundation of the State of New York, the Florida State University, and Temple University have enabled us to devote our summers to explorations of various aspects of state courts. We are particularly indebted to the Social Science Research Council for a grant to conduct research on the judicial role in four states.

Our old friend and former colleague, Herbert Jacob, participated in early explorations of state courts while at Tulane University and has continued to give his encouragement and counsel. Bradley Canon and Glendon Schubert have shared their thoughts with us on various aspects of the state judiciaries, and Kenneth Dolbeare commented on a first draft of this work.

We record a debt of gratitude to the supreme court judges of Louisiana, New Jersey, Massachussetts, and Pennsylvania who not only consented to interviews, but in many instances talked to us openly and at length about their positions as judges. Judge Albert Tate, now of the Louisiana Supreme Court, has furnished us the rare opportunity of discussing state courts and the roles of judges with a sitting judge who himself has written about many of the problems that concerned us. Judge Tate found time in a very busy schedule to correspond

with us at length about the activities of state court judges; he also read the
initial draft of this work and made many valuable suggestions and correc-
tions. Rarely has a work had such intellectual opportunities furnished by
one of the objects of study.

We have not always followed the suggestions made by our colleagues and
critics but have preferred to go our own way; such an intellectual route
places the responsibility for all aspects of this work where it belongs—upon
the authors.

Finally, we recognize the staff of Prentice-Hall who tendered the opportunity for this publication and exercised great patience and understanding
during its completion. Roger Emblen guided the work to completion and
Maurine Lewis, Marianne Sturman, Ellen Frei, and Rosalie Creswick worked
with us in smoothing out the rough edges.

HENRY ROBERT GLICK

KENNETH N. VINES

STATE COURT SYSTEMS

1 THE STUDY OF STATE COURTS

All states—the poor and the small, the large and the wealthy—conduct elements of state politics through judicial institutions. Yet of the three branches of state government, state judiciaries have been the least investigated, and are therefore the most poorly described in political science. For example, general works on state politics usually treat courts according to legalistic conceptions, or else describe them in the simplest structural and formal terms. Only quite recently have scattered studies examined state courts in political terms.[1]

Although many factors have inhibited the political analysis of state courts, a leading cause has been their inadequate conceptualization and location in political theory. We intend to examine judicial institutions in the American states, utilizing the most appropriate theoretical conceptions and analytical techniques available in political science. In this chapter we shall establish the theoretical and conceptual setting by which courts may be investigated as effectively as the legislative and executive institutions of state government have been. First we suggest the theoretical orientation by which state courts can be considered as political institutions. Second, we suggest the conceptual framework that can

[1] Representative works are summarized in Herbert Jacob and Kenneth N. Vines, "State Courts," in Herbert Jacob and Kenneth N. Vines, eds., *Politics in the American States*, rev. ed. (Boston: Little, Brown and Company, 1971).

most effectively delineate judicial institutions; finally, we deal with judicial inputs and discuss how these affect the courts.

COURTS AS VALUE ALLOCATORS

Looking to modern political theory, we can see that we need to adopt a new orientation toward the study of state courts in order to bring them within the framework of modern political analysis. Specifically, we need to interpret judicial activities in terms of power, allocation of values, political behavior, and decision making, in order to link judicial analysis more closely with contemporary political science. For example, Harold Lasswell has stated that politics involves "who gets what, when, how,"[2] a conception that seems inappropriate when applied to courts. Courts are generally not featured in the mass media as focal points of power struggles or of political controversy in the states. Occasionally, however, conflicts in court activities are just as intense and have stakes just as high as those in other aspects of state politics. Studies of the courts of Michigan, Louisiana, and Pennsylvania have revealed highly volatile political struggles within the judiciary involving great amounts of power and resources that have been allocated by the courts.[3] Because judicial activities are not commonly publicized and their political conflicts are deemphasized, the courts are often passed over in public perceptions of state politics.

While legislatures and state executives quite visibly distribute resources in the form of appropriations, welfare bills, and executive appointments, judicial allocation of values is much less obvious, and we may sometimes find it difficult to conceive of state courts as centers of political power having influence in policy making. We do not maintain that judicial institutions are necessarily as important as legislatures and governors in state politics; however, the determination of their role is an empirical problem that should be investigated in different situations and at different times. Only then can we chart the position of the courts in state government.

Justice Brennan, who served on the New Jersey Supreme Court before his elevation to the United States Supreme Court, has provided some valuable insights on state courts as value distributors.[4] He stated that state courts have greater significance than the federal courts, observing that "the composite work of the courts of the fifty states probably has greater significance in measuring how well Americans attain the ideal of equal justice for all." Specifically, Brennan views the importance of state judiciaries as residing in their provision for "vital issues of life, liberty, and property." State courts delve deeply into important values of American life in handling cases dealing with business relationships and property rights;

---

2 Harold Lasswell, *Politics: Who Gets What, When, How* (New York: Whittlesey House, 1936).
3 For examples see Henry Robert Glick, *Supreme Courts in State Politics* (New York: Basic Books, Inc., Publishers, 1971).
4 William J. Brennan, "State Supreme Court Judge Versus United States Supreme Court Justice: A Change in Function and Perspective," *University of Florida Law Review*, 29 (Fall 1966), 225–37.

essential issues of family life, such as divorce, adoption, wills, trusts, and estates; labor relations; consumer rights; and most criminal prosecution. Although most of these cases do not make the headlines, they involve the basic issues and problems of daily life and affect many basic personal and social values in American society. From this perspective, the role of courts in the distribution of values becomes clear.

One reason why value allocations in state courts are difficult to identify is that they are carried out by means of distinctive legal orientations that set them apart from the remainder of state politics. The legal culture consists of sets of attitudes and behaviors toward all activities in the courts, many of which are not visible to the public. Procedures involved in bringing a case to court, the conduct of trials, and decision-making processes are highly formal, and are controlled and presented in legal language and symbols not commonly used in other political activities in the states. A calm, ritualistic, and respectful atmosphere dominates most judicial activities. In contrast to these legal orientations, democratic orientations to politics often support a populistic style and language that result in more open and highly publicized activities in state legislatures, local politics, and aspects of the executive. Because judicial behavior is usually carried on in legal terms rather than according to the democratic orientations associated with much of state politics, the political functions of state courts tend not to be as easily recognized as those of the other components of the state political system.

COURTS IN THE STATE POLITICAL SYSTEM

To realize our objective of examining judicial institutions in the states, we shall use the conceptual framework of the political system presented and advocated in political science by David Easton.[5] Judicial politics refers to all activities involved in the authoritative allocation of values by the courts. According to systems theory, all events in political life are conceived as a series of interdependent events that interact in sequential fashion. By considering state courts in a systems framework we can delineate political functions of the state courts that might otherwise escape our attention. Important concepts of systems theory that will guide our identification of the essential elements of judicial politics include *inputs, conversion processes, outputs, outcomes, and feedback.*

Inputs

The sequential series of activities in the political system begins with inputs. Inputs include demands made of the system or support given to it; they are channeled into the system through political institutions, one of which is the judiciary. Demands are made of most institutions by groups or

---

[5] For a more extended treatment of the application of systems theory to the study of state politics, see Jacob and Vines, *Politics in the American States,* Chap. 1.

individuals through such activities as petitions, letters, personal contacts, and other means that we normally associate with political parties or with organized interest groups. In courts, demands are made mostly through the formal process of litigation by groups or individuals who bring cases for adjudication.

Support is given the courts through favorable attitudes concerning judges and their activities, and also through appropriations and provision for court facilities. There is some evidence, such as low turnout for judicial elections, that popular support for the judiciary tends to be passive and covert. Interesting evidence of support for the courts is the material resources afforded them. The money appropriated each year for the courts is meager indeed.[6] During 1967–1968 the average per capita expenditure of all states for their courts was $1.03; only 6 states spent more than $3.00 per capita, and 26 spent less than $1.00. Nor were the capital expenditures for court facilities any greater—all of the states spent only $2.8 million for capital improvement in the same period. In contrast, capital outlays for the police in 1967–1968 were $37.3 million (presumably representing money spent primarily on police stations and equipment). Clearly, material support tends to be minimal and not actively promoted, probably in part because courts do not have an active corps of lobbyists and partisans promoting their interests in state capitals.

Conversion processes

The processes that transform inputs into policies are termed the conversion processes. The most common source of conversion in the courts results from litigation and ensuing case decisions. Judicial conversion processes are much less visible than those of legislatures, where traditions have developed which promote considerable public exposure of the decision-making process. In contrast, judicial decision making takes place in great secrecy. Jury deliberations are hidden from outsiders, including the judge presiding at the trial, and appellate judges produce their decisions in conferences closed to all observers. Political scientists who study processes of judicial decision making are hampered by the emphasis on secrecy that pervades much of the judicial process. Nevertheless, although the inputs and decision-making processes are somewhat different for courts than for other agencies, the courts are directly involved in the conversion process of state government.

Outputs

The decisions made by the courts are termed outputs. These are the means by which courts meet demands and make policies. Judicial policies are by no means confined to judges alone, but also result from decisions reached by other officials such as police, prosecutors, sheriffs, and attorneys throughout the criminal and civil processes, beginning at points before the cases are tried. By far the best known outputs of the courts are controversial

---

[6] State and Local Government Studies No. 55, *Criminal Justice* (Washington: Bureau of the Census, 1970), 11.

decisions made by the highest appellate courts, particularly the national Supreme court and, to a lesser extent, the state supreme courts. But the kinds of strict or lenient decisions produced in traffic courts involving drunken drivers, or in municipal courts with regard to slum landlords, are examples of the fact that other court decisions, despite their lack of publicity, also are outputs of the political system.

Outcomes

Effects of judicial decisions that extend beyond the immediate value allocations and have long-range social and economic effects are what we term outcomes. For example, strict judicial enforcement of traffic laws and traffic judges who are severe with drunken drivers could materially affect safety on the highways. On the other hand, arbitrary and unequal judicial decisions could lead to such outcomes as attitudes critical of American justice and reduced confidence in the courts.

Feedback

Although systems theory conceptualizes a sequence of events including inputs that lead to conversion processes which, in turn, lead to outputs and outcomes, the political system is by no means static or unidirectional. Feedback is the term given to the manner in which the outputs and conversion processes affect the inputs and the resulting interactions. Court policies may themselves result in increased inputs or demands on the courts. For example, if judges interpret divorce laws leniently, more persons may file for divorces, with resulting increase of inputs; if courts declare acts of the legislature unconstitutional, persons who object to legislative enactments may be encouraged to turn to the courts to secure remedies.

JUDICIAL INPUTS

Because inputs begin the activities of the courts, we shall discuss them more fully. However, research in this area is limited; therefore, our treatment of inputs can be only suggestive. Our treatment is basically twofold. Although we shall discuss many familiar partisan pressures that affect courts, as well as other institutions, we shall also emphasize legal orientations that are especially significant in the judicial process. By viewing both sets of demands together, we can provide a more complete view of inputs affecting state courts.

A major reason that state courts seem somewhat apolitical is the low visibility and relative lack of salience of their inputs. Compared to those that we observe in the state legislatures and executives, the demands, claims, and requests made in the courts usually appear rather minor. As political institutions, the courts seem passive, their publics acquiescent, and their activities of little general concern.

Identification of judicial inputs is difficult because they require close observations and their qualifications must be carefully specified. An excellent way to emphasize judicial inputs is to compare courts and other state agencies in their response to pressures. In order to view courts from the same perspective as other institutions, we shall deal with such inputs as recruitment, interest groups, political parties, and public opinion.

The organization of courts and selection of judges are important in describing the setting and actors of judicial activity, but they are also special areas of input activity. Interest groups which have stakes in court decisions and judges' behavior tend to deal somewhat more openly with issues that cluster around judicial organization and recruitment. (Because of both the visibility and importance of pressures in the operation of courts, we treat judicial organization and selection in separate chapters.) The recruitment of judges (if we follow systems theory that regards recruitment as an input) is the most obvious and well-documented phase of the inputs of state courts.

Constraints on judicial inputs

Although all political institutions have certain limitations placed on their activities, the constraints on judicial inputs are unusually restrictive. Three types of limitations for circumscribing the inputs of courts are most prominent:

(1) Judicial ethics: A highly moralistic series of statements designed to restrict the activities of judges in politics was adopted by the American Bar Association in 1922 and amended several times since then.[7] The canons of judicial ethics have been endorsed by nearly all the states, sometimes by bar associations and judicial conferences, and also are found in certain legislative acts. However, the effect of judicial ethics on judges' activities is unknown. Although other state agencies such as legislatures are concerned with political ethics, we assume that judicial ethics restrict judges' activities more effectively than most. We believe that these ethics may be an important part of the state judicial role and that values held both by judges and members of the public circumscribe inputs in the courts. Judicial ethics warn judges away from contact with political parties, interest groups, elections, and other kinds of participation.[8] Moreover, we assume such values inhibit interest groups in their contacts with courts, except for questions involving judicial recruitment and organizational forms.

(2) Politics by litigation: Except for those of judicial recruitment and organization, issues raised before the court involving state politics must be in the form of litigation. Although there is scope for a certain amount of ingenuity, politics in the form of litigation does tend to be restrictive because of the formal requirements it customarily includes. Few states allow

---

[7] Susan A. Henderson, *Canons of Judicial Ethics* (Chicago: American Judicature Society, 1969). This publication reprints Canons of Judicial Ethics and gives a history and commentary on Judicial Ethics. Also included is a list of states and methods of adoption of the Canon of the ABA.
[8] Glick, pp. 60–62 and Chap. 6.

advisory opinions, and litigation is usually carried out by specialists. If a group or faction has no lawyers or very poor ones, its access to the courts via litigation may be hampered or prevented entirely.

(3) Politics by others: It is a distinctive characteristic of litigation that judges cannot initiate suits no matter how concerned or informed they may be about certain issues or problems. This means that judges lack the power to raise issues or initiate policies in their own political institutions. The effect is to place judges in a rather passive position and prevent policy activities even within the bounds of judicial ethics. Although this passive role is implied in the concept of litigation, the helplessness of judges deserves special emphasis.

Public opinion

Because state judges are usually natives of the district or state of their courts, we assume that they are aware of their neighbors' opinions. Moreover, they are cognizant of the reactions of the mass media, such as newspapers, television, and periodicals, to the issues of the day. Compared to the activities of the legislature and governor, however, the mass media generally finds judicial proceedings, with some exceptions, not newsworthy and devotes little space to them. Scattered evidence suggests that political movements sometimes include references to courts and judges[9] but, as a whole, the general public finds the actions of courts less interesting than those of other state institutions. However, we really know little about the relationship of state judges to public opinion because the problem has rarely been explored.

Interest groups

David Truman, a prominent theorist of interest groups, states that courts "are one of the points at which the claims of interest groups are aimed."[10] Except for some investigations of judicial selection and organization, there have been few studies to test Truman's theory.

The constraints present in the courts quite probably both obscure and limit interest group activities. Indeed, in the usual sense of the term, lobbying, with its connotations of informal interactions and communication, is hardly possible in the courts. Seldom is it regarded as being within the bounds of propriety to "buttonhole" judges, to call upon a judge in chamber, or to begin a letter or telegram campaign. For these reasons, we seek other evidence of group activity in the courts.

The best documented phase of group activity in the national Supreme Court, the support of litigants by amicus curiae briefs, has not been

9 On state courts and public opinion see: V. O. Key, Jr., *Public Opinion and American Democracy* (New York: Alfred A. Knopf, 1961), pp. 4–5; Jack Ladinsky and Allan Silver, "Popular Democracy and Judicial Independence," *Wisconsin Law Review*, No. 1 (Winter 1967), 128–69.

10 David Truman, *The Governmental Process* (New York: Alfred A. Knopf, 1951), p. 497.

explored in the states. A fundamental difficulty is that we really have little information as to whether the potential for such briefs exists in the states.

Although amicus curiae briefs have not been systematically described, there is evidence to confirm Truman's observations concerning other activities of groups in the state courts. The studies of Glick, Vose, and Sayre and Kaufman[11] show that despite the limitations, groups can be identified in litigation. Certain groups, namely those concerned with zoning, fair trade regulations, education, and civil liberties, appear to be particularly prominent in the state judiciaries.

In general, however, interest groups appear less vigorous in their activities and less concerned with courts than with other agencies of state government. This lack of concern reflects in part the presence of constraints and in part the limited resources available to the courts for policy making. (For example, courts have no direct power over the purse either in appropriating monies or in imposing taxes but can influence financial policies only indirectly through settlements.) Yet, courts can be innovative in policy making perhaps because they are less directly affected by interest groups and public opinion. (For example see *Serrano* v. *Priest*,[12] a decision by the California Supreme Court that would change the fundamental method of financing education in the states.)

Attention was called to the activities of interest groups in state courts when the national Supreme Court dealt with an issue arising out of the activities of the NAACP. Although Virginia, in common with most other states, prohibited barratry (the legal equivalent of ambulance chasing or the stirring up of litigation for profit), the Court held that NAACP activity tried to make litigation possible by providing encouragement, expert services, and legal advice for groups lacking these. In that case, *NAACP* v. *Button*, the Court recognized the importance of group activity in litigation by conceiving of litigation as a political freedom protected by the Fourteenth Amendment and stating specifically that litigation "is . . . a . . . form of political expression."[13] The Court's opinion also pointed out that groups will turn to the courts when their efforts have been unsuccessful elsewhere in state politics.

Political parties

The absence of major party activities in the courts calls attention to one of their most striking contrasts with other state agencies. Although the expression and mobilization of partisan values is accepted as normal and necessary in the legislatures and executives, they are peripheral to activities in the state judiciaries.

Many state judges have been party activists before their recruitment and often are selected for partisan reasons. Once on most courts, however, a

---

[11] Glick, Chap. 6; Clement E. Vose, "Interest Groups, Judicial Review, and Local Government," *Western Political Quarterly,* 19 (March 1966), 85–101; Wallace S. Sayre and Herbert Kaufman, *Governing New York City* (New York: Russell Sage Foundation, 1960), Chap. 15.
[12] Serrano v. Priest, Sup. 96 Cal. Rptr. 601.
[13] NAACP v. Button, 9LEd. 2nd 416 (1965).

combination of judicial ethics, effective insulation, and the formalities of litigation tends to separate judges from parties. Even while campaigning for office, the judge is only indirectly in contact with other partisan campaigns occurring at the same time. Insulation from political parties is maintained on the courts where there is no visible manifestation of partisan pressures. Judges are not organized, as in the legislature, along party lines; party whips or other control devices are not used, and judges are not expected to take an active part in party affairs.

Yet studies have revealed a correlation between judicial behavior and party values.[14] With the relative absence of linkages, the relationships between partisan values and judicial behavior may seem mysterious unless the functions of party identification are recalled. Before selection for the judiciary the typical judge identifies with a party and strengthens partisan values by activities and associations within it. On the court, as before selection, judges meet critical issues involving questions of liberty, property, security, and authority. Although the language and symbols of the law disguise many issues in litigation, most judges probably have little difficulty in recognizing the presence of these critical values. For example, a judge who has been a liberal Democrat might be inclined toward the prolabor side in workmen's compensation cases. Similarly, Republican judges may tend to decide in favor of business interests.

LEGAL INPUTS IN STATE COURTS

As we indicated above, one of the distinctive features of the judiciary is that activities on all levels, including inputs, conversion processes, and outputs, are usually presented in terms of legal symbols, legal vocabulary, and formal legal processes. Although there are legal influences in other state agencies—such as the language and method of drafting legislative bills and certain administrative procedures—legal orientations permeate every aspect of judicial institutions.

Although legal orientations are particularly identified with courts, they compete with other orientations, especially democratic orientations, for dominance in the judicial subsystem.[15] Democratic orientations emphasize such values as popular control and maximum public interactions, and are advocated by political parties and other groups which are vehicles of popular control over political institutions. Throughout American political history, advocates of popular control have urged democratic orientations be adopted in the operation of state courts, and such episodes were particularly important in the effects of Jacksonian democracy and the nonpartisan movement on state judicial systems. Contemporary political parties often lead the way in urging democratic orientations in the operation of certain features of state courts.

[14] For a representative selection and summary of such works see Jacob and Vines, eds., *Politics in the American States*, Chap. 8.
[15] Democratic and legal orientations toward the courts are discussed more fully in Richard J. Richardson and Kenneth N. Vines, *The Politics of Federal Courts* (Boston: Little, Brown and Company, 1970), Chap. 1.

Legal orientations are maintained by legal groups in the states such as bar associations, judicial councils, and legal educational groups. Although there are some differences among legal groups, they generally agree in advocating that every phase of the judicial system be conducted according to nonpartisan conceptions, that the courts be independent of both governmental and public linkages, and that the courts be insulated from the pressures of group activity and public opinion. Often nonlegal groups join in the advocacy of legal orientations, but legal groups generally furnish the leadership.

Legal orientations occur in the fundamental training and socialization of participants in the judicial process. Attendance at law school imbues students, who later staff the courts and handle the input processes as attorneys, with a vocabulary and set of concepts used to handle litigation. In addition, persons appointed as judges are further socialized through experience on the court and contact with other judges. Legal groups such as the American Bar Association (ABA) establish plans that are measuring rods for legal orientations in state courts. For example, the ABA has offered model plans for both the selection of judges and the organization of courts in the states. The plans, which tend to maximize legal orientations and minimize partisan values, are, in turn, advocated by state groups; many states have responded by adopting plans approximating the ABA models.

A primary channel for maintenance of legal orientations is the litigation process. Demands fed into the judicial conversion process are presented according to the formal requirements of the legal case method, and decisions are made in the vocabulary and structure of legal concepts. An exception occurs in decision making that takes place before cases reach trial. Pretrial decisions, such as those made by a district attorney not to prosecute, or to accept a guilty plea to a reduced charge, involve informal bargaining and negotiation which is not limited by strict legal rules and procedures.

The measuring rods for democratic orientations are rarely formalized, but can be found in the ideas of popular reform movements and institutions. Democratic orientations are evident, for example, in such instances as the Jacksonian movement to reform the courts and to elect judges. In common with other state institutions, courts bear the marks of democratic experimentation and reform to bring them closer to popular control. Indeed, democratic orientations in the courts are deeply rooted in American political history. Postrevolutionary state governments reacted against colonial experiences by shortening the terms of judges and providing for their election by state legislatures rather than appointment by governors. Later, Jacksonian democracy brought increased popular control through heightened partisan activities in the judiciary and the election of judges in partisan elections. The Progressive movement sought to bring a still greater measure of popular control to the courts through nonpartisan elections and recall of judges. This was intended to remove organized political party control of the selection of judges, thereby providing the voters with more direct influence over recruitment and judicial decision making. Like the federal courts, state judiciaries experience continuous political conflict reflecting, in part, the tensions between legal and democratic orientations. Consequently, one of the main themes in state politics is the conflict between legal and democratic groups which seek influence in aspects of judicial politics.

Demands for revision of the courts according to legal specifications are an increasingly major input into the political system. Legal groups have been particularly interested in securing changes in the method of judicial selection, reform of court organizational structures, and provisions for professional administrative and research staffs in the work of the courts. In some states these groups have been quite successful in getting their reforms adopted, but in others they have made little progress. Consequently, there is much variation in the extent to which the judiciaries of American states embody legal orientations.

We have measured the extent of legal orientations in state court systems through the construction of a composite index which includes several aspects of state courts.[16] A high score indicates the adoption of legal orientations for major aspects of the state's judicial system; a lower score indicates fewer legal orientations. Our critieria for the identification of legal orientations in court systems are the positions taken by the ABA or other legal organizations for such aspects of judicial politics as judicial recruitment, court organization, and judicial administration.

The scores of the 50 states, presented in Table 1-1, indicate a vast range in the extent to which legal orientations are present in state courts. California, with the highest score of legal professionalism, outscore Mississippi, the lowest, by a ratio of seven to one. Most of the states with the highest scores—California, New Jersey, Illinois, Massachusetts, New York, Michigan, and Pennsylvania—are the large industrial, urban states; most of the states at the lower of the continuum tend to be southern states. Indiana seems a surprising exception, since it is the only large industrial, urban state with a low ranking of legal professionalism.

The scores in Table 1-1 are not to be interpreted as indicating the absolute presence or absence of legal orientations, but rather as denoting their dominance in certain critical aspects of court judicial politics, such as judicial selection and court organization and administration. All court systems in the American states have in common a certain minimum legal culture that characterizes the input and decision-making aspects of the judicial system.[17] Mississippi, with the lowest score, differs from California

---

[16] Our index of legal professionalism is a composite score including five major factors of state court systems. The factors include (1) method of selection for judges in all courts—states were scored for approximation to ABA model plan of selection; (2) states court organization and the approximation to the ABA model court structure; (3) judicial administration in the states—states were scored for presence of professional administrator and size and nature of his staff; (4) tenure of office for judges of major trial and appellate courts and approximation to ABA recommendations; (5) level of basic salary for judges of major trial and appellate courts exclusive of fees and local payments. Each factor involved scoring the states on a five-point scale according to how closely judicial features in the state approached the ABA model.

[17] Even Louisiana, with traditions stemming from the French Civil law, has adopted most features of other state judicial systems. See George A. Pope, "How Real Is the Difference Today Between the Law of Louisiana and Most of the Other Forty-Seven States?" *George Washington Law Review,* 17 (February 1949), 186–89.

TABLE 1-1   LEGAL PROFESSIONALISM IN
THE AMERICAN STATES

Rank of states	Composite score
1. California	21.7
2. New Jersey	18.0
3. Illinois	17.7
4–5. Massachusetts, New York	16.7
6–7. Alaska, Michigan	16.3
8–9. Maryland, Hawaii	15.3
10. Pennsylvania	15.0
11–13. Colorado, Washington, Wisconsin	14.3
14. Ohio	14.0
15. North Carolina	13.7
16. New Hampshire	13.4
17–19. Arizona, Oregon, Rhode Island	13.3
20. Nevada	13.0
21. Connecticut	12.6
22–24. Idaho, Minnesota, Oklahoma	12.0
25. North Dakota	11.3
26. Kentucky	11.0
27. Iowa	10.9
28–29. Maine, Wyoming	10.7
30. Vermont	10.3
31–33. Florida, Montana, Virginia	10.0
34–36. Delaware, Louisiana, Missouri	9.6
37–38. New Mexico, Utah	9.3
39–40. Nebraska, South Dakota	9.0
41. South Carolina	8.7
42–45. Georgia, Kansas, Tennessee, Texas	8.0
46. Indiana	7.6
47. West Virginia	7.3
48. Alabama	6.0
49. Arkansas	5.3
50. Mississippi	3.4

mainly with respect to the degree of legal orientations in the judicial system, but this degree is important and makes the California courts different from the Mississippi judiciary in major ways. Like California, Mississippi processes all demands through litigation shaped by formal legal procedures and legal traditions, but the two court systems diverge with regard to many important procedures.

In general, California has responded to the pressures of legal professionalism, while legal groups in Mississippi have failed to reform the states' courts according to modern legal specifications. For example, California selects judges by a nonpartisan plan in which legal groups have a strong voice; Mississippi still elects judges in partisan elections adopted during the Jacksonian period. California pays its judges more and allows them longer terms in office. In addition, California's court structure follows closely the ABA model for rational, simplified organization, while Mississippi retains aspects of a more confusing court organization and has paid little heed to professional legal recommendations. Finally, California has a system of judicial administration including a professional court administrator aided by a research and administrative staff, while Mississippi has no professional judicial administration, not even a court administrator. The result is that California courts are molded in critical ways by legal groups and operate in an environment of legal professionalism. Mississippi's courts, on the other hand, have hardly been touched by modern legal orientations and retain many features of nineteenth-century political orientations toward the courts.

In subsequent chapters we shall examine important problems of the state judiciaries suggested by the role of courts in the political system. First we investigate the organization of courts to determine the structure within which demands made of the judiciary must be channeled. Both legal groups and democratic groups have been active in making demands concerning the way in which they believe the courts should be organized. Next we consider the selection of judges, looking particularly at legal and democratic inputs. Demands and pressures surrounding the judicial selection process are probably the most visible arena of inputs into the judicial system. A consideration of the judicial role in the American states follows. Chapter 5 deals with decision making in state courts and considers some of the important aspects of court conversion processes. Finally, we examine the outputs of the judiciary by considering judicial policies.

II STATE COURT ORGANIZATION

The organization of state courts is more than an adjunct of rational legal theory and recognition of "needs for change." Questions of court organization involve various groups that have interests in the courts and seek ways to influence the structure of the judiciary to satisfy their own demands. Thus demands for court organization are important inputs into the political system.

There are various reasons why state court organization may become a controversial political issue. First, state courts have opportunities to make meaningful policy decisions, and their powers, structure, and functions are important to individuals and groups concerned with judicial decisions. The structure of court systems also has important implications for the way decisions are made and the opportunities provided for individuals to use the courts. In addition, state courts provide valuable posts which are sought by political parties and allied interest groups for allocation as patronage rewards for party workers and supporters. Finally, the structure of state courts is crucial to lawyers and judges, who make their living in the judiciary. Changes in court rules and procedures, consolidation of courts, and changes in jurisdiction all directly affect the routine practice of law and the jobs of judges.

The aims and interests of all of these groups frequently differ; however, they are linked to one another in that they focus upon certain features of judicial orga-

14

nization which each considers crucial. This results in serious political conflict, with outcomes that vitally affect the structure of the state judiciary. In this chapter we shall discuss the conflicts over court organization, the development and variations in court structures, and their political implications in the 50 states.

THE POLITICS OF STATE COURT ORGANIZATION

Although state court systems have grown in order to meet new political demands made on judicial decision making, most states have retained some features of older judicial institutions. Traditions have been difficult to escape, and state courts reflect a combination of the old and the new.

One prominent result of this sporadic and unplanned growth is the political conflict which frequently erupts between advocates of court change and reform and opposing groups who favor maintaining the status quo. This conflict is important politically because it concerns differences in the values and stakes of different groups in the structure and behavior of state courts.

Courts added to state judicial systems are designed to perform needed judicial functions, but they also satisfy the demands of political parties and allied interest groups for additional political jobs (patronage) to be filled by party and group supporters. In addition, once they are established, the courts become part of the decision making machinery of state and local governments, and have the power and opportunities to make decisions satisfying or denying various political demands. Thus, after new courts are added and begin to function, it is often difficult for changes to be made because of the investments of various groups in the existing system.

Proponents of court reform have different interests in the judicial system. Motivated by legal and judicial ideals—and different political goals—they favor improving the efficiency of state courts by reorganization of parts or all of state court institutions. For example, they frequently propose scrapping certain trial courts whose functions overlap those of other courts, and they favor changing the jurisdiction of various courts in order to clarify the purposes and powers of all state courts. This is intended to overcome the confusion and delays which confront litigants and lawyers when they seek to initiate a suit in the proper court. Court reformers also frequently advocate removal of state courts from the influence of partisan politics in order to enable judges to make decisions objectively. To accomplish this goal, they favor selection of judges by nonpartisan lawyer/laymen commissions instead of by popular election.

Proposals for court reform generally come from the leaders and activists of state and local bar associations.[1] National organizations such as the ABA, the Institute of Judicial Administration, and the American Judicature Society collect information and publish proposals for court reform, but

[1] Much of the following discussion is derived from Lois Morrell Pelekoudas, "Judicial Reform Efforts in Ten States, 1950–1961" (Ph.D. Dissertation, University of Illinois, 1963).

generally do not become directly involved in the politics of court change in individual states or cities. Thus, while many ideas for court reform have originated within national organizations, specific attempts to modify court structures take place on the state level.

Advocates of court reform have been successful in some states, but even their victories in contests for change often have come only after long and heated political struggles. In early attempts to have changes adopted, leaders of the bar worked in isolation from other groups who might have become interested in court reform. As a result, bar associations were easily rebuffed by state legislatures not inclined to listen to the ideas of a small group of men who were not representative of broader community interests.

Recent efforts at reform, however, have involved many different groups, for lawyers desiring change have realized that they need allies to help them circulate ideas about court reform and to press for the necessary legislative action or referenda that will implement their proposals. Supporters of court reform usually come from outside the ranks of political party organizations or state legislatures. The lawyers involved are most often the more successful, wealthier, often predominantly Republican attorneys who practice in the cities. They become involved in court reform partly because court inefficiency is frustrating and a potential threat to their practices. Equally important, however, they become active because of indignance about what they consider to be "political" or partisan links between city courts and political parties—most frequently the Democratic party, which controls many city administrations. They are supported by middle class organizations which also favor a "businesslike" approach to good government, removing the influence of political parties and doing away with "special favors" for "special interests." Such groups as the Parent-Teachers Association, League of Women Voters, American Association of University Women, the American Legion, chambers of commerce, church federations, and real estate associations often participate.

The opponents to court reform vary depending upon the specific proposals, but generally they come from individuals and groups which have the greatest stakes in the existing system. Proposals which call for abolition of the justice of the peace or other local trial courts of limited jurisdiction, for example, will usually motivate incumbents of these positions to organize strong opposition. Allied with others who oppose changes for their own reasons, they can be a powerful force in persuading legislatures to retain the status quo. They also may actively campaign against passage of a referendum that will decide the issue.[2] Other opponents may include urban Democratic political party leaders who are against a decrease in the number of judges or courts and plans for lawyer-dominated selection commissions. If court structures and recruitment systems change, they fear they will lose their influence on judicial selection. Moreover, since proponents for change are often the more successful Republican attorneys, the Democrats believe that more Republicans will be chosen and that conservative business

---

[2] See, for example, David Mars and Fred Kort, *Administration of Justice in Connecticut,* ed. I. Ridgway Davis (Storrs, Conn.: Institute of Public Service, University of Connecticut, 1963), p. 28.

interests will dominate the courts. Therefore, they fight to protect their own interests. In Chicago, for instance, the Democrats were successful in forcing acceptance of a compromise state court reform proposal (which failed to win voter approval in a referendum) that did not affect the selection procedures in Cook County, thus preserving Democratic dominance in judicial recruitment.[3] Minority groups and labor also often oppose the commission form of selection because they believe their members will get fewer court posts than they do in party dominated elections, where building a winning ticket usually requires ethnic group and labor representation. The less prominent attorneys, who generally are not members of large law firms, but have private practices often devoted to representation of small clients against large companies (e.g., insurance claims), also oppose selection procedures that will choose conservative, Republican judges not responsive to the interests of their clients.[4] They also feel that few of their number will receive court posts.

Reasons other than loss of political patronage and fear of unfavorable court decisions motivate other groups to oppose court reform. Many rural lawyers and legislators often see nothing wrong with the courts in their county, and therefore see no reason to change the system. Unlike city courts, their courts' dockets are not overflowing, and large political party organizations which dominate important facets of city politics do not exist. Moreover, they are accustomed to their courts and the way they function and do not want to have to learn new trial procedures in new courts.[5]

These kinds of reactions to court reform proposals are not limited solely to rural areas, for even some lawyers in cities feel so attached to the established methods that they are reluctant to agree to changes. A case in point concerned the use of pretrial conferences in New Jersey. Arthur. T. Vanderbilt, a prominent national spokesman for court reform and leader of reform in New Jersey, found it difficult to persuade lawyers and large companies involved in extensive litigation to make more efficient use of pretrial conferences. The conferences are designed to speed trials by giving the opposing attorneys the opportunity to agree to the veracity of certain evidence and testimony, making full presentation in court unnecessary. At first the attorneys believed that the conferences would simply add to the time they had to spend on each case, and therefore reduce the amount of litigation they could handle. However, when shown that each case would in fact take less time, thus enabling them to handle more cases, they finally agreed to the change. The large companies which spent great sums on lawyers' fees also agreed when they were convinced that each case would require much less time, thus freeing millions of dollars kept in reserve for the settlement of cases.[6]

3 Gilbert Y. Steiner and Samuel K. Gove, *Legislative Politics in Illinois* (Urbana: University of Illinois Press, 1962), pp. 189–90.
4 Richard A. Watson, Rondal C. Downing, and Frederick C. Spiegal, "Bar Politics, Judicial Selection and the Representation of Social Interests," *American Political Science Review,* 56 (March 1967), 54–71.
5 Mars and Kort, *Administration of Justice in Connecticut,* p. 32.
6 Arthur T. Vanderbilt, *The Challenge of Law Reform* (Princeton: Princeton University Press, 1956), pp. 65–67.

Lawyers may also oppose court reform because they feel that the existing system maximizes their opportunities for gaining court hearings and winning their cases. Charges of this form of lawyer opposition to court change occurred in New York, where the judges of the Court of Appeals (the state's highest appellate court) sought major alterations in the court's jurisdiction. Arguing that the New York Court is the most overburdened supreme court in the United States, the judges tried to persuade the legislature to decrease the variety of cases which the court must decide and, instead, to give the judges themselves greater discretion in determining which cases they will hear. This would have meant placing limitations on the right of appeals, and would have decreased the workload of the court.

Instead of granting their request, however, the state legislature made only minor changes in the court's jurisdiction. In response to this defeat, one judge stated that the bar was largely responsible for the position taken by the legislature. He explained that lawyers oppose drastic changes in the court's jurisdiction because:

They like to keep all the cases coming here. They're not sure they've really lost the case until they have it actually decided by the final court.[7]

If the right of appeal is granted to a great variety of cases, the judicial process generates more and extended litigation. The loser can seek additional points of access within the judicial system and hope for a victory at some point on the appellate ladder.

Despite opposition to change, one survey of reform efforts has shown that eight of ten proposals in ten states were adopted. Seven concerned structural changes in the courts, and three established a commission form of selection for certain judges. One selection proposal and one structural proposal each were defeated.[8] Reform proposals are often successful, it seems, because compromises are frequently reached between the major supporters and opponents of change, so that both sides ultimately endorse a modified proposal that goes before the voters. Even compromises not directly connected to court reform may be included. In New Jersey, for example, the Mayor of Jersey City campaigned successfully on a statewide basis against constitutional revision which included court reform until he won concessions for proposed tax revisions which would guarantee higher taxation of railroad property in his city.[9]

THE DEVELOPMENT OF STATE COURT SYSTEMS

As we have mentioned, state traditions are important factors in accounting for the structure of current court systems. However, while certain traditions persist, state courts also have changed over time in response to various

---

7 *The New York Times,* 24 November 1969, p. 50.
8 Pelekoudas, "Judicial Reform Efforts in Ten States, 1950–1961," pp. 2–3.
9 Ibid., p. 49. For more on New Jersey Court reform see Kermit Wayne Smith, "The Politics of Judicial Reform in New Jersey" (Ph.D. Dissertation, Princeton University, 1964).

political pressures. Competing demands have come from various sectors of the political system, and although they have varied in different historical periods, political conflicts over the structure of state courts have existed from the creation of judicial institutions in America. To understand the character of current court organization and the links between courts and other political agencies, we shall examine some of the main currents of state court development and the political demands associated with them.

Colonial courts

State courts have evolved from rather simple institutions during the colonial and early postrevolutionary period to very complex, highly specialized court systems. Figure 1-1 depicts the growth of state courts from early American history to the present. In the colonial period most political power was centralized in the colonial governor and his immediate advisors. With few exceptions, the governor performed executive, legislative, and judicial functions. Certain minor officials were appointed by him to aid in managing judicial duties, but they exercised little independent power.

In the early period of colonial rule the tasks of governing were relatively simple and routine. Since there were few people gathered in small settlements, there was less need for extensive formal political institutions that became necessary as the population increased and social and economic relations grew more complex. As the population increased, new courts were created to provide local agencies for settling an increasing number of conflicts. These few new courts were organized on the town and county levels so that the litigants would not have to travel great distances to have their cases argued.[10] Appeals from all courts usually could be taken to the governor and the assembly, and ultimately to the courts of England, but this occurred only rarely; in most instances the governor and the assembly had final judicial authority.

The judicial and legal systems developed differently in each colony, depending upon local beliefs and customs. The English common law tradition and English court structures generally were adopted, but were soon modified to suit the requirements of local demands. Religious practices and customs as well as the commercial development of the individual colonies resulted in different legal rulings and court structures.[11] In certain respects, these early variations among the colonies have persisted and contribute to the great variety of court systems today.

The structure of colonial courts and the development of law were also affected by the general absence of legal experts. Lack of well-trained lawyers reflected the low status of law and the courts in the early colonial period, and was a factor as well in perpetuating the nonprofessional image of the judiciary. Few lawyers emigrated to the colonies;[12] moreover, court pro-

---

[10] See, for example, Mars and Kort, *Administration of Justice in Connecticut,* pp. 20–21.
[11] Francis R. Aumann, *The Changing American Legal System* (Columbus, Ohio: Ohio State University, 1940), pp. 6, 10.
[12] Ibid., p. 8.

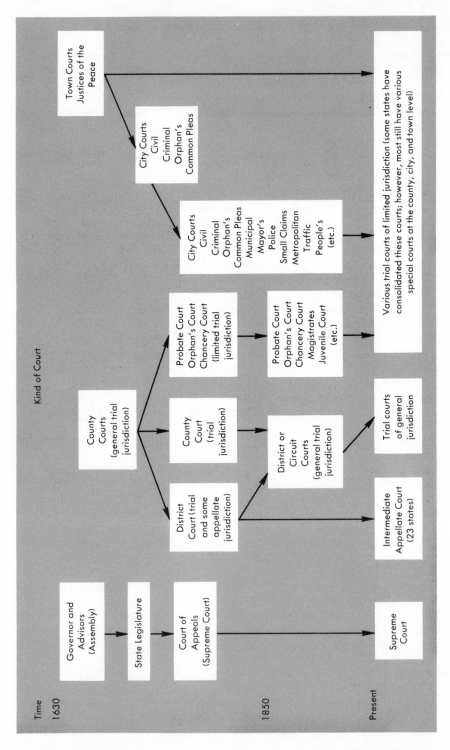

FIG. 1-1. The evolution of state courts.

cedures and the law in England were distrusted by the colonists, many of whom had come to America specifically to escape legal action. Therefore, they were not sympathetic to the development of a professional class of lawyers in America. Wealthy landowners and merchants also opposed the development of a professional bar because they feared competition for the general social, economic, and political control which they exercised over colonial society.[13]

As a result, early courts were staffed on a part-time basis by laymen with little or no legal training.[14] The judges generally were merchants, planters, and wealthy landowners who gave part of their time to settling local disputes. In terms of political control, judicial power coincided with the influence of business and other financial interests on life in the colonies.

Despite the absence of trained personnel and the unpopularity of law and the judiciary, new courts continued to be added to the judicial system in response to increasing and varying demands. Population growth and the expanding economy increased the amount of litigation, and more courts were required to dispose of the cases (Fig. 1-1). As early as 1685, the General Court of Massachusetts, which performed legislative functions as well as trial and appellate court duties, was so overburdened with cases that magistrates of each of the county courts were permitted to act as judges in certain cases formerly decided by the General Court.[15] In 1691 a new court of Chancery was created and given jurisdiction over these cases. Similarly, in 1698, Connecticut established probate courts which dealt specifically with wills and estates, a group of cases formerly heard by the county courts.[16] As new kinds of courts were added, judges and lawyers dealt with more specialized cases, thereby gaining skills and establishing rules and procedures that further differentiated judicial and legislative institutions. Although the courts did not become politically independent for some time, the distinction between legislative and judicial functions contributed to the eventual development of larger judicial systems and a separate base of political power resting in the state courts.

Early American courts

After the revolution, the powers of the governor were drastically reduced, and in their place state legislatures exercised much more political influence. State courts, however, were distrusted as much as before. The memory of English courts sustained a belief among the colonies that judicial action was coercive and arbitrary. Since colonial courts usually were controlled by the governor as extensions of his power, the colonists were not anxious to see the development of a large, independent state judiciary. As a result, there was no great change in the structure of the judiciary immediately after the Revolution. Moreover, judicial decisions were scrutinized by state

[13] Charles Warren, *A History of the American Bar* (Boston: Little, Brown and Company, 1911), p. 8.
[14] Aumann, *The Changing American Legal System*, p. 35.
[15] E. H. Woodruff, "Chancery in Massachusetts," *Boston University Law Review*, 9 (1929), 169.
[16] Mars and Kort, *Administration of Justice in Connecticut*, p. 22.

legislatures, and judges sometimes were removed or a particular court abolished to counter the effect of an unpopular court policy.[17] A case in point occurred in Pennsylvania, where several judges were impeached for sentencing a man to jail for contempt of court. The impeachment was justified by the belief ". . . that punishment for 'contempt' was a piece of English common law barbarism, unsuited to this country."[18]

Distrust of the judiciary became even more prevalent when various courts declared legislative action "unconstitutional." Unlike many English practices which were modified and adopted in the colonies, judicial review of legislative action was largely an American innovation. Shortly before the Revolution, it was used on occasion by the courts to justify opposition to colonial edicts. However, judicial review became most important after the Revolution, and was a major source of political conflict between courts and legislatures. Despite threats and actual removal of judges in a few instances, the courts became more assertive and declared legislative acts unconstitutional with greater frequency. These cases often involved major economic interests, such as state policy governing creditor-debtor conflicts. The legislatures were usually more responsive to a freer money policy favoring debtor interests, while the courts reflected the demands of creditors who urged a strict policy in the collection of debts. In several instances, state courts declared unconstitutional legislative acts favoring free money.[19]

These early political conflicts between state courts and legislatures were significant for court organization, for they were an indication of the eventual development of an autonomous judicial system. Although certain state legislatures continued to perform an appellate judicial function for many years,[20] state courts were beginning to establish the basis of independent judicial authority. Also, as we have indicated, courts and law became more specialized as the population increased and the economy of the states developed. This also contributed to the emergence of state courts as independent political institutions.

Courts in a modernizing society

The structure of state courts, caseloads, and decisions began to change in important ways in the mid and late 1800s. This period of industrialization in the United States brought about changes not only in business and economic relations, but also changes which affected the fundamental char-

---

17 Herbert Jacob, "The Courts as Political Agencies," in *Studies in Judicial Politics,* ed. Herbert Jacob and Kenneth N. Vines, Tulane Studies in Political Science, Vol. 8 (New Orleans: Tulane University, 1962), p. 17.
18 Aumann, *The Changing American Legal System,* p. 80.
19 Jacob, "The Courts as Political Agencies," p. 18. While Marbury v. Madison is well known as the United States Supreme Court case in which the high court proclaimed its power to review legislation, eight state courts had espoused the power of judicial review years before the famous 1803 case. See Charles Grove Haines, *The American Doctrine of Judicial Supremacy* (Berkeley: University of California Press, 1932), pp. 148–65.
20 Legislative appellate power ended entirely in the United States in 1857, when Rhode Island transferred all appellate judicial authority to the state supreme court. See Aumann, *The Changing American Legal System,* p. 164.

acter of American life. Labor unions were formed in increasing numbers, immigrants from Eastern and Southern Europe began to arrive in the cities of the northeast, and the trend toward modern urban society began. These changes created pressures which never had been felt before: Life styles which were so much an integral part of a largely rural United States began to be replaced by new structures, new attitudes, and new expectations in an industrial nation. Like other institutions, the courts were also affected by these fundamental revisions in the patterns of American society.

Industrial technology such as the development of steam power and the growth of railroads, shipping, and commerce were the source of conflicts that had not existed in simpler times. New kinds of litigation over rates charged, liability for personal injury to passengers and damage to the property of shippers, as well as questions concerning the basic structure of corporations, were channeled into the courts. In many instances legislation dealing with such problems did not exist, and the courts had the responsibility of creating new rules which would cope with questions of the industrial age. Such responsibilities provided the courts with opportunities to make important public policy and to establish state courts as necessary parts of the political system.[21]

The growth of business law also furthered the professionalization and specialization of the practice of law. Lawyers had occupied a superior social status from colonial days, and were important in engineering the revolution and forming the structure of the federal government. Despite their social status, however, lawyers were distrusted by the general public, which viewed them as shrewd but corrupt and greedy men who took unfair advantage of the uninformed.[22] These views contributed to early state laws limiting or outlawing the practice of law. Nevertheless, as the export trade, slavetrading, and fishing expanded, merchants found increasing need of legal experts who could draw proper documents and were familiar with the growing body of court cases which served as precedents in litigation. A legal profession was required, and laws forbidding the professional practice of law began to disappear. There also developed a greater opportunity for individuals to obtain legal training.[23] When corporations were formed and expanded, technology made commercial relations even more complex, and there was even greater need for legal expertise. Law eventually emerged as both a prestigious and a necessary occupation.

In addition to the professionalization of law, the industrial revolution brought about many profound changes in the structure of local courts. Coastal cities grew in the 1800s with the expansion of commerce, and new courts were created specifically to meet the needs of the growing cities (Fig. 1-1). Often, courts similar to those already existing at the county level were created especially for city litigation. However, these courts proved inadequate for meeting the unique problems created by the vast population shifts to the cities in the post Civil War period.

---

21 See, for example, Warren, *A History of the American Bar*, pp. 475–507.
22 James Willard Hurst, *The Growth of American Law* (Boston: Little, Brown and Company, 1950), p. 251.
23 Warren, *A History of the American Bar*, pp. 16–17.

Simply the *amount* of litigation generated from large concentrations of people was a new pressure on the judicial system, but more important were the new situations which earlier courts, operating in a more simple, rural society, had never had to consider. The closeness of city living, the requirements of grueling industrial employment, and the influx of many different social groups affected the traditional life patterns of the new city dwellers. Adjustments to an often bewildering environment were difficult to make, and family cohesion and self-sufficiency were seriously undermined. Relations between tenants and landlords, and between employees and employers, frequently led to conflicts and court suits. Shattered family life, juvenile delinquency, and higher crime rates were also problems with which the courts had to deal.

Minor conflicts between consumers and small businesses also generated much litigation. Earlier business litigation had usually involved larger corporations, but the growth of the cities provided a setting for the establishment of many small retail businesses. Disputes between businesses and between buyers and sellers were often petty and relatively unimportant in terms of broader social or political developments, but they were important to the litigants themselves, and city courts were faced with many new demands. Finally, the widespread ownership of automobiles posed numerous problems. Traffic laws had to be created by legislatures and interpreted by the courts; accident claims and the development and application of liability law placed more demands on courts.[24]

These new demands had a major impact on the structure of state court systems. Although the number and variety of state courts had grown somewhat in the past, social and economic change occurred so rapidly toward the end of the nineteenth century that most state judicial systems could not meet and satisfy the demands made upon them. For a time existing city courts, primarily Justices of the Peace, dealt with much of this new litigation, but the structure of these courts was unsuited for this purpose. Most of the judges had little or no training and lacked the ability to do more than simply process the cases as best they could. Moreover, the fee system of justice courts often made it very expensive for an individual to make a claim. Typical cases included employees' claims for wages, collection of small debts, and payment for sold goods. The amount of money involved was often less than $50, but the fees charged by the court sometimes could take 10 per cent or more of the amount collected—a figure that many claimants could not afford.

In response to these complex problems, some states began to enlarge their judicial systems by adding new courts whose jurisdictions, procedures, and personnel were designed to deal with specific parts of the new litigation. Not only did these new courts help to dispose of many cases, but, more significantly, they represented innovations in judicial structures and ways of coping with social and economic pressures. One important change, for example, was the creation of small claims courts with simplified

[24] Hurst, *The Growth of American Law,* pp. 147–69.

procedures and the absence of lawyers, intended to help in the collection of debts at minimal cost. Juvenile and family relations courts also were added in some cities. Besides settling litigation, these courts attempted to provide some constructive guidance to the juvenile offender and the troubled family. As early as 1869, courts in Illinois began to consider the young lawbreaker not as a criminal, but as a ward of the court who needed special corrective action.[25] Later, social workers, psychiatrists, and other personnel were added to provide additional services. Similarly, traffic courts were added in many cities to manage the litigation resulting from increased automobile ownership.

Additions of new courts and judges to state judicial systems generally were not made according to any overall coherent plan for the state judiciary. Changes were sporadic and haphazard, and little attention was paid to jurisdictional boundaries—the possibility that the authority of one court might overlap with that of another. In addition, except for the power of appellate courts to review the decisions of trial courts, each court was an independent institution. Rules of procedure and decisions themselves varied widely; judicial decision making was highly decentralized.

The sheer number of courts and the complexity of jurisdiction which resulted from expansion of the judiciary are often extremely difficult to understand. A 1931 study indicated that Chicago had 556 independent courts, 505 of which were Justice of the Peace courts. Other state and local courts included municipal courts, circuit court, superior court, county court, probate court, juvenile court, and criminal court. Other courts, such as the Rackets Court, sometimes were added to deal with special problems. The jurisdiction of these courts was not exclusive; i.e., a case could be brought before a variety of courts depending on the legal and political advantages that each one offered. Since many courts, including the justices of the peace, had countywide jurisdiction over many similar kinds of cases, the alternatives open to attorneys were vast.[26]

Factors such as court costs, the decisional reputation of the judge, speed of securing a decision, and the complexity of court procedures were considered in determining which court to use. For example, depending on the stakes, a prosecuting attorney in a criminal case could choose a court which was likely to produce either a harsh or lenient judgment. Other attorneys sought to have their cases entered in courts whose procedures were so complex that they would entangle and confuse the opposition in legal technicalities. Moreover, partisan political considerations were also involved, for the many justices of the peace, who competed for fees, were often eager to trade favorable decisions for court business.[27]

Complexity of court structure exists in many states. A description of Maryland's judicial system commented, for example:

---

[25] Ibid., p. 155.
[26] Albert Lepawsky, *The Judicial System of Metropolitan Chicago* (Chicago: University of Chicago Press, 1932), pp. 19–23.
[27] Ibid., pp. 43–62.

Maryland's court system is very complex. There are no less than 16 different types of courts, with little uniformity from one community to another. A lawyer from one county venturing into another is likely to feel almost as bewildered as if he had gone into another state with an entirely different system of courts.[28]

Despite the addition of new courts, many state court systems seem unable to meet the increasing demands placed on judicial decision making. Numerous courts have extensive backlogs of cases waiting to be heard. For example, in Pennsylvania, the Allegheny (Pittsburgh) and Philadelphia County Courts were created to shift part of the burden of a heavy caseload from the Courts of Common Pleas (trial courts of general jurisdiction) in Pittsburgh and Philadelphia. However, congestion and delay are still common in these city courts. Recently, there was an average delay of three and one-half years in many civil cases going to trial in Philadelphia; other cases had been delayed for as long as four and one-half years. In Pittsburgh, a city smaller than Philadelphia and one with *more* judges, there was an average delay of two years, eight months, with some cases waiting almost six years to move through the trial courts.[29]

Backlogs are also common in criminal courts. This was demonstrated dramatically in 1970 in New York City when approximately 4500 prisoners in the city's five largest jails rioted and seized hostages in order to express numerous grievances. One of their major complaints concerned delays in the city courts which prevented them from receiving speedy trials. Since many of the prisoners were poor, they were unable to pay bail to gain their release pending trial and consequently were held in jail until their cases were called. A survey of delays showed that prisoners were held without trial an average of 91 days, but some had been waiting six months or a year in jail. One prisoner, charged with murder, had been awaiting trial for three years.

Many city and state officials recognized the legitimacy of the prisoners' grievances and called for reforms which would speed up the work of the courts. Few specific proposals were made, however, and one state judge remarked that the problem really did not involve the courts, but simply demonstrated the need for more jails to alleviate crowded conditions which lead to riots.[30]

The issue of delay in the courts is common among lawyers and judges who urge improvements in the general efficiency of state courts. However, delay also has several political implications, one of which concerns the success of interest groups in achieving their objectives via political action. There are numerous points of access which groups may use in their attempts to influence governmental policies which affect their interests. Legislatures, executive officials, and administrative agencies, as well as the courts, are

---

[28] *Survey of the Judicial System of Maryland* (New York: Institute of Judicial Administration, 1967), pp. 11–12.
[29] A. Leo Levin and Edward A. Woolsey, *Dispatch and Delay* (Philadelphia: University of Pennsylvania Press, 1961), pp. 12–15.
[30] *The New York Times,* 2–7 October 1970, p. 1.

alternative avenues in the pursuit of favorable governmental decisions. For example, business, labor, or civil rights organizations may attempt to influence congressional or state legislative policy, or try to effect the enforcement (or nonenforcement) of state and federal statutes. They may also try to achieve their goals by initiating suits against government officials or others who oppose them. They may be unsuccessful in some of these actions, but if one point of access is closed to them (i.e., they do not obtain favorable decisions from a particular agency), they may seek alternative courses.

However, if litigation is their technique, there is not only the possibility of an unfavorable court decision, but delay itself works against the group. Since a court decision may be postponed for months or years, the litigants are forced to wait before realizing their objectives. In turn, delay gives an advantage to those who oppose changes in current policy.

Delay also affects individuals who become involved in conflicts which cannot be settled privately, and for which no avenue other than a court suit is available. Much litigation in the state courts, for example, concerns suits for damages brought by persons who have been injured in automobile accidents, on the job, or on the premises of various businesses. In order to collect compensation for their injuries, the litigants must be prepared to contend with delays which may mean years of waiting before their case comes to trial. Witnesses of the accident may die or move away during this time, and memories of exactly what happened to cause the accident may dim. Moreover, litigants may become tired and frustrated with the slowness of the judicial process, and may even abandon their attempts to collect compensation, or settle for whatever an insurance company or business is willing to offer. However, even if they withstand the burden of court delays and win the case, the losing party could appeal the decision and the period of waiting would begin once more.

Delay in the judicial process contributes to a strategy used by defendants in civil suits to escape financial obligations, in which they try to transfer their cases to a court with a large backlog of litigation in order to postpone court decisions which could go against their interests. Moreover, in areas where all or most of the courts have long delays, the possibility of going to court may convince a plaintiff to settle his claim privately and for less than he might hope to receive by waiting for a trial. These conditions suggest that citizens who must use the courts to settle civil disputes have little confidence or trust in a governmental institution whose procedures do more to frustrate than to facilitate their efforts at obtaining justice.

The political implications of dissatisfaction with criminal court procedures are particularly compelling, as seen from the New York riots. The riots appeared to be well organized and ably led, but, more important, the grievances expressed by the prisoners and the tactics they used to gain attention were very sophisticated. Prisoner leaders demanded meetings with prison, city administration, and court officials as well as live television and newspaper reportage of their complaints. Their grievances also reflected considerable awareness of issues that are basic to concepts of justice in the

United States. This sophistication is especially significant since many prisoners were poor Puerto Ricans and Blacks, and many were illiterate and poorly educated. The ability of prisoner leaders to focus widespread attention on basic problems concerning state court procedures suggests that court organization will become an even more important political issue as organized demands continue to be made for improved court operations and a higher quality of justice in the United States. Coupled with other contemporary protests about social and political injustice, the judiciary may become a more visible and controversial target of political action.

The present organization of state courts

All 50 states have three general tiers of courts: state appellate courts (courts of last resort and intermediate appellate courts) whose main function is to review decisions of lower courts, state trial courts of general jurisdiction, which have the broadest scope of authority in holding trials, and various specialized local trial courts of limited jurisdiction which generally hear minor cases. Certain of such courts, for example, hear only cases involving traffic violations, wills, or very small sums of money.

Although the basic structure of state court systems is similar, the specific number, names, and functions of state courts vary widely. Table 2-1 lists the types of courts and describes how they vary among the states. The major differences are in the presence or absence of intermediate appellate courts and the great variation in the number and types of trial courts of limited jurisdiction. The states are similar in that most have only one or two types of trial courts of limited jurisdiction. The combination of type and number

TABLE 2–1   STRUCTURE OF STATE COURT SYSTEMS

Supreme Court
All states have one supreme court. In some states this court in termed the Supreme Judicial Court or Court of Appeals.

Intermediate Appellate Courts
23 states have intermediate courts of appeals. Oklahoma, Tennessee, and Texas have 2 intermediate courts of appeals, 1 each for civil and criminal cases. Intermediate appellate courts have various names: Superior Court, Court of Appeals, Appellate Division of Supreme Court or Superior Court, Superior Court.

Trial Courts of General Jurisdiction
38 states have 1 type of trial court of general jurisdiction, 9 states have 2, 2 states have 3, and 1 state has 4. The names of these courts vary widely: Circuit Court, Superior Court, District Court, Common Pleas, and, in New York, the Supreme Court.

Trial Courts of Limited Jurisdiction
8 states have only 1 or 2 of these kinds of trial courts; 10 states have different kinds; 20 states have 4 or 5; 12 states have 6 or more different kinds. The names and functions of these courts vary widely. They include: Probate Courts, Justice Courts, Police Courts, Small Claims Courts, City and Town Courts, Juvenile Courts, Orphan's Courts, Courts of Oyer and Terminer, and Courts of Chancery.

Sources: State Court Systems (Chicago: The Council of State Governments, 1966); *Martindale-Hubbell Law Dictionary, 1970; Intermediate Appellate Courts* (Chicago: American Judicature Society, 1967).

TABLE 2–2   **CONTRAST OF STATE COURT SYSTEMS**

California	Florida
	Appellate Courts
Supreme Court	Supreme Court
District Courts of Appeals	District Courts of Appeals
	Trial Courts of General Jurisdiction
Superior Courts	Circuit Courts
	Court of Record (Escambia County only)
	Trial Courts of Limited Jurisdiction
Municipal Courts	Civil Court of Record
Justice Courts	Criminal Courts of Record
	Civil and Criminal Court of Record
	Courts of Record
	County Judges' Courts
	Juvenile and Domestic Relations Courts
	Small Claims Courts
	Justice Courts
	Municipal Courts
	Metropolitan Court

of courts contributes to court systems which vary from the very simple, with jurisdiction clearly defined, to highly complex systems having numerous trial courts of limited jurisdiction whose functions frequently are unclear and may overlap with one another. Variations in the complexity of court systems are apparent in the contrast between the courts of California and Florida, as shown in Table 2-2. Both court systems are modern in that both have intermediate appellate courts. However, the Florida court system is much more complex than that of California because it has two trial courts of general jurisdiction and many more trial courts of limited jurisdiction.

As we discussed earlier, many efforts have been made to change complex and frequently inefficient court systems into more modern, streamlined structures. One proposal for change, sponsored by the ABA, calls for creation of a state court system having only four courts: a supreme court, an intermediate appellate court, one type of trial court of general jurisdiction located in various districts throughout the state, and a set of magistrate's courts which would have jurisdiction over less important cases not heard by the district courts.[31]

In order to indicate their relative complexity, as well as the extent to which each of the state court systems is traditional or modern, we have classified them according to the particular characteristics of the system. The classifications have been derived by contrasting each court system with the characteristics of the model judicial system favored by the ABA. The distribution of the states along a continuum ranging from simple and modern to complex and traditional court systems is shown in Table 2-3.

Only North Carolina has adopted the ABA's model system; it took the place of the state's much more complex system in 1971. However, other

[31] "ABA Model State Judicial Article (1962)" *U.S., Task Force Report: The Courts* (Washington, D.C.: U.S. Government Printing Office, 1967), pp. 92–96.

TABLE 2–3 DIFFERENCES IN STATE COURT ORGANIZATION[a]

Simple and Modern ←		→ Complex and Traditional	
Group 1 $N = 6$	Group 2 $N = 20$	Group 3 $N = 20$	Group 4 $N = 4$
*Arizona	*Alabama	Connecticut	*Arkansas
*California	*Alaska	Idaho	Delaware
*Illinois	*Colorado	Iowa	Mississippi
*North Carolina	*Florida	Kansas	Virginia
*Oklahoma	*Georgia	Kentucky	
*Washington	Hawaii	Maine	
	*Indiana	Massachusetts	
	*Louisiana	Minnesota	
	*Maryland	Montana	
	*Michigan	Nebraska	
	*Missouri	New Hampshire	
	Nevada	North Dakota	
	*New Jersey	Rhode Island	
	*New Mexico	South Carolina	
	*New York	South Dakota	
	*Ohio	*Tennessee	
	*Oregon	Utah	
	*Pennsylvania	Vermont	
	*Texas	West Virginia	
	Wyoming	Wisconsin	

*States marked with an asterisk have intermediate appellate courts.

[a]In order to place the states in one of the four groups distributed along the continuum, they were given a weighted score according to the specific characteristics of the court system. The higher the score, the more simplified and modern the court system. The score was computed as follows:

A. A court system is considered simplified and modern if it has one intermediate appellate court, but more complex if it has two or more types of intermediate appellate courts. It is considered much less modern, however, if it has no intermediate appellate court. Therefore, each state received:

4 points for having one intermediate appellate court
3 points for having two or more types of intermediate appellate courts
0 points for having no intermediate appellate court

B. The fewer types of trial courts of general jurisdiction which a state has, the more modern and simplified its court system is considered to be. Therefore, each state received:

2 points for having one trial court of general jurisdiction
1 point for having two types of trial courts of general jurisdiction
0 points for having more than two types of trial courts of general jurisdiction

C. The fewer types of trial courts of limited jurisdiction which a state has, the more modern and simplified its court system is considered to be. Therefore, each state received:

3 points for having one trial court of limited jurisdiction
2 points for having two types of trial courts of limited jurisdiction
1 point for having three types of trial courts of limited jurisdiction
0 points for having more than three types of trial courts of limited jurisdiction

The score for each state is the sum of its scores in sections A, B, and C. Scores ranged from 1 to 9. The scores included in each group are: Group 1—7, 8, 9; Group 2—4, 5, 6; Group 3—2,3; Group 4—1.

states closely approximate this model: Arizona, California, and Washington have a supreme court, an intermediate court of appeals, one type of trial court of general jurisdiction, and *two* trial courts of limited jurisdiction. The court systems of the other states in Group 1 are also simplified. At the other end of the continuum we find states with no intermediate appellate courts, two or more trial courts of general jurisdiction, and four or more trial courts of limited jurisdiction. Most of the states, however, lie between these two poles; their court systems are more complex in basic structure than those in Group 1, and some have intermediate appellate courts while others do not.

Several major political implications are posed by the structure of state judicial systems. First, it is important to note that although the courts are presented in Table 2-1 as part of a judicial hierarchy, with the state supreme court as the highest court and the trial courts of limited jurisdiction as the lowest, there are various reasons why decision making is important at each level of the judicial system. Relatively few cases are appealed to higher courts, which means that the decision of the trial court is the one and only decision to be applied. For example, the Florida Supreme Court disposes of approximately 1000 cases per year. It decides only about 450 of them with formal written opinions. The district courts of appeal (intermediate appellate courts) decide about 3000 additional cases. However, the circuit courts (trial courts of general jurisdiction) dispose of almost 100,000 cases in a single year, while the other trial courts in the state decide over 400,000 cases.

Court decisions made at various levels of the judicial hierarchy are significant, not only because of the large number of cases involved, but also because we cannot assume that only important cases are appealed. The decision to appeal depends a great deal on the financial resources of the litigants and their ability to endure the pressures and uncertainty of possible years of waiting until their case is heard and the final decision rendered. Many people apparently are willing to allow the decision of the lower courts to be the final resolution of the case.

It should also be recognized that the appellate process does not necessarily involve all levels of courts in a single case. Table 2-1 would seem to suggest that appeals travel from various trial courts through an intermediate stage before they are heard by state supreme courts. However, unlike the federal judicial system, where this generally is the process, many state cases go directly from trial courts to state supreme courts, bypassing the intermediate appellate level. Certain other cases which are heard by intermediate appellate courts cannot be heard by state supreme courts due to restrictions on the jurisdiction of the high court. This means that although certain courts are designated as intermediate appellate courts, they may, in effect, be state courts of last resort. These characteristics of state court systems further highlight the significance of all courts in the judiciary as important decision-making institutions.

Although relatively few cases are appealed from the court in which they originate, the structure of state court systems does permit the interaction of several different courts in settling a particular case. An important feature of the judicial process is that every litigant generally has the right to at least one appeal. The court to which a losing litigant may appeal varies depending on the court of origin (whether the case comes from a trial court of limited or general jurisdiction) and on the specific character of the case itself (e.g., the amount of money involved in the suit, the seriousness of the crime for which the defendant has been convicted, or the field of law governing the case). As stated before, the decision to appeal must be made by the litigants themselves, but at least there is an opportunity to seek a new hearing by a higher court. When this occurs, judicial decision making involves several stages, with at least one, and sometimes several, additional courts taking part in determining the final outcome. Thus the judicial system decentralizes the locus of decision making and provides numerous opportunities for policy making to occur.

The presence of many different kinds of courts also means that several alternatives exist for seeking judicial action. As mentioned above, the functions of trial courts of limited jurisdiction frequently overlap in complex judicial systems. This multiplies the potential number of participants in judicial decision making and provides litigants and attorneys with alternative points of access into the courts and avenues of appeal within the system. Various courts operating under different rules and having judges with different attitudes and policy preferences may be used or avoided as part of a strategy of litigation designed to achieve one's own goals and confuse and defeat opposing interests. When court systems are simplified, these alternatives are less numerous.

The organization of state court systems has additional implications for relationships among state courts. The presence of many locations where judicial policy making can take place means that the decisions of appellate courts may conflict with those handed down by trial judges. According to legal theory, because trial courts are "lower" courts in the judicial hierarchy, they are obliged to follow the lead of appellate ("higher") courts by altering their own policies if they differ from those adopted by higher courts. However, there are few controls which an appellate court can impose on the lower courts to insure that its policies are adopted. Therefore, except when supreme courts overturn specific decisions, trial judges are generally free to make decisions according to their own judgments, thereby creating the possibility of conflicting judicial policies in the state. This condition also underscores the importance of all courts in the judicial hierarchy as significant policy-making bodies.

In addition to their independence in policy making, other features of state judicial systems permit most courts to be autonomous. In about half of the states, supreme courts have authority to make certain rules regulating the entire state judicial system.[32] These rules may determine such things as procedures to be followed in conducting trials or appellate hearings, or may even permit the chief justice of the state supreme court to transfer judges to other jurisdictions if the caseload of the courts is unevenly distributed throughout the state. Certain state supreme courts appear to exercise considerable power over judges throughout the state court system. The New Jersey Supreme Court, for example, has a rule which prohibits judges from participating in any political campaigns. Although the court does not have the power to remove a judge from office, some judges feel

---

[32] See individual state constitutions and "Rule-Making Power of the Courts," (New York: Institute of Judicial Administration, 1962); "The Judicial Rule-Making Power in State Court Systems" (Chicago: American Judicature Society, 1967).

that violation of this rule very likely would result in the resignation of a lower court judge if requested by the supreme court.[33] This places restrictions on judges in that particular state, but does not seem to be a common practice throughout the United States. Most supreme courts have only partial rule-making power, and the extent to which they are able to impose restrictions on the courts varies. In general, it appears that most rules made by supreme courts affect specific court procedures only (e.g., the time limit placed on filing appeals and motions), and that judges throughout the state are able to act without significant administrative interference from other courts.

Since the actual operation of most state judicial systems does not make state judges part of a well-regulated, cohesive hierarchy, each court can be viewed as a separate point of access where various pressures are brought to bear. First, judicial decentralization and autonomy make it possible for courts to become integral parts of local political systems. They must deal with litigation reflecting local social, economic, and political conflicts, and their decisions have the potential of establishing important policies affecting local practices in such areas as zoning, taxes, education, conduct of elections, and governmental regulation of business.[34] The policy-making role of local courts is less visible and proceeds differently from that of city councils, mayors, or boards of education; however, courts deal with problems similar to those facing other local decision makers. Moreover, the relatively easy access afforded various local interests to a variety of courts places the judiciary well within the structure of local decision making.

The proliferation of largely autonomous courts also provides political parties with numerous opportunities to use the judiciary as a source of patronage for party supporters. Judgeships are prestigous positions which are attractive to many lawyers. In return for financial contributions and work in political campaigns, certain attorneys are supported by party organizations and other local officials for recruitment to the courts. In this way, the parties repay a political debt and obtain continued support by local judges.[35]

STATE COURT SYSTEMS
AND THEIR SOCIAL ENVIRONMENT

Numerous pressures account for variations in the basic structure and complexity of state court systems. In addition to the interests of political parties and competition between interest groups, judicial systems reflect the social environment in which they exist. For example, as the states increased in population and more people began to live in large cities, more judges and newer courts were added to the existing judicial system. There is a close correlation between the size of a state's population and the number of

---

[33] See Henry Robert Glick, *Supreme Courts in State Politics* (New York: Basic Books, Inc., Publishers, 1971), pp. 123–27.

[34] For a discussion of policy making in trial courts, see Kenneth M. Dolbeare, *Trial Courts in Urban Politics* (New York: John Wiley & Sons, Inc., 1967).

[35] Wallace S. Sayre and Herbert Kaufman, *Governing New York City* (New York: Russell Sage Foundation, 1960), pp. 522–57.

judges on the trial courts of general jurisdiction ($r = .87$). This high correlation means that, generally, as state populations increase from less than 1 million to approximately 20 million, the number of judges on the major trial courts also increases.

We can view this relationship from several perspectives. First, the addition of judges to a judicial system is a response to the changing requirements of a society. However, this change also reflects a shift in certain basic demands made on the political system which, in turn, have implications for the scope of government and its policy outputs. Before the period of industrialization, the United States was primarily an agricultural society in which personal relationships were stable and relatively simple. Most conflicts were not very complex and could be settled informally and privately between friends and neighbors. However, when industrialization and urbanization occurred, many simple and familiar social structures were replaced by more complex, tenuous, and less secure ones. Resolution of conflicts became more difficult, partly because they occurred increasingly between strangers and involved more diverse and complicated issues (e.g., automobile accidents, employee and other personal injury suits and insurance claims, business transactions, property transfers). In place of private settlements, conflicts became the source of new demands channeled into the political process and, as in other institutions of government, the scope of the judiciary broadened along with increases in the size of the judicial system.

In addition to the relationship between number of judges and population of a state, we would hypothesize that the number of trial courts of limited jurisdiction in a state would be related to the percentage of the population residing in urban areas. Our hypothesis is derived from the general tendency in most states for new, specialized courts to be added when urbanization increases and new problems become the basis for increased demands on the judicial system. It is striking, therefore, to discover that there is *no* relationship between these two variables. The number of different types of trial courts of limited jurisdiction differs among the states, but the variation is not related to measures of urbanism in each of the states. This requires some explanation.

State court systems have expanded with increases in population and special courts have been added in many cities to deal with new urban problems. However, as indicated above, since the 1940s the court systems in a number of states have been modernized and the number of different types of courts reduced in an effort to streamline the judiciary and make the functions of each state court more distinctive. This has occurred in some highly urbanized states, but not in others. California, for example, has two types of trial courts of limited jurisdiction even though the state is 86.4 per cent urban. New York is almost as highly urban (81.4 per cent), but has nine different types of trial courts of limited jurisdiction. A similar situation exists in states which are less highly urbanized. Georgia and Montana, for example, are similar in the percentage of the population which resides in urban areas (55.3 and 50.2 per cent respectively); yet Georgia has six different types of trial courts of limited jurisdiction, while Montana has only three.

While there is no relationship between urbanism and the number of trial courts of limited jurisdiction, there is some indication that the more highly urbanized states are more likely to have intermediate appellate courts than states with a smaller percentage of urban population. Referring to Table 2-3, we note that the average percentages of urban population for the states included in Groups 1 and 2 are 68.7 and 67.8, respectively. All but four of the 26 states in these two groups have intermediate appellate courts. In contrast, the average percentages of urban population for the states in Groups 3 and 4 are 55.7 and 50.3, and only two of these 24 states have intermediate appellate courts.

Addition of intermediate courts usually resulted from the heavy work-load carried by the state supreme courts. Faced with increasing litigation, generated primarily from large urban areas, judges and various reform groups have argued for an additional court to screen out much of the litigation formerly heard by the state's highest tribunal. However, unlike the many trial courts of limited jurisdiction, which resulted in a proliferation of courts and new demands for consolidation, the creation of one or, in a few states, two intermediate appellate courts did not create conflicts over consolidation or revision of appellate courts. Therefore, we continue to find a relationship between percentage of urban populations and presence of intermediate appellate courts.

Besides the effects of urban growth and political movements to reorganize the courts, state court systems reflect the political and social history of the state. As discussed above, state court systems frequently are combinations of old and new judicial institutions, for the significance of tradition and continuity with the past are probably more important for courts than for other governmental agencies. This reflects a commitment to stability in the law and the emphasis which courts usually place on the rules, legal theories, and procedures used in the past as sources of guidance in current decision making. Several courts in certain states—primarily those in the east with a longer history—still bear the same names and some of the functions of courts in the colonial and postrevolutionary era. Probate courts, orphan's courts, courts of chancery, courts of common pleas, and justices of the peace have existed throughout the history of the United States. The western states tend to have more modern and simplified state court systems. Since they were settled and incorporated into the Union relatively recently, they lacked the strong political and legal traditions that shaped many features of governmental institutions in the older states. In the west, governmental organization was more closely matched with the contemporary needs of the state. Thus, judicial institutions were simplified and modernized, making them relevant to the times.

III THE JUDGES: THEIR SELECTION AND BACKGROUND

In contrast to legislators and governors, all of whom are popularly elected, state judges are chosen by a variety of means. This variety is reflected in the history of states' selection systems and in the participants who have influenced adoptions and changes. Judicial selection has been responsive to democratic opinion, but it has also reflected the forces of state traditionalism, partisan politics, and legal professionalism. Historically, some state selection systems have maintained post-revolutionary state practices, while others have been influenced by contemporary democratic reform movements or legal innovations. Participants in the shaping of state selection systems include political parties, reform groups, state political elites, and also such legal professional groups as bar associations and judicial conferences. Only the influence of civil service is missing; unlike most European systems, the American states have never developed civil service systems for their judiciary.

Judicial selection takes place in an environment relatively free of legal constraints. Although codes of ethics and tradition urge that activities such as campaigning be kept within bounds, the severely controlled atmosphere of the courtroom is lacking. As a consequence, the process of judicial selection admits most of the range of inputs that occur in state politics, and the relative lack of insulation permits a clear view of these forces. Because of the variety of participants and the relative absence of legal constraints, judicial selection is a major channel for inputs into state court systems.

IMPORTANCE OF JUDICIAL POSITIONS

Among all positions in state government, judgeships are particularly prized. Some reasons for their importance are: (1) number of positions available; (2) salary level; (3) favorable conditions of tenure; (4) prestige of office; and (5) character of work.

Including major trial courts and appellate courts, in 1969 there were 5,087 judgeships distributed in the 50 states, an average of 101.7 for each state.[1] Each state had from three to nine supreme court justices, 23 states had varying numbers of intermediate appellate judgeships, and each had a number of trial judges, resulting in a great disparity in the number of judicial positions in the states. For example, although Alaska had only 16 such judicial positions available, 5 appellate and 11 trial court judgeships, Illinois had 641, including 31 appellate and 610 major trial positions. Other states with large numbers of judicial posts were California with 471, New York with 256, and Texas with 262. In general, number of judgeships seems associated with size of the state's population, but another relevant factor is the character of the state's judicial system. For example, New York is more populous than Illinois, yet Illinois had in 1969 more than twice as many judgeships (641) as did New York (256); the reason is that New York has adopted a streamlined judicial system which eliminated many judicial positions.[2] Next to members of the state legislature (an average of 152.4 per state), there are more judgeships in the states than any other type of significant political office.

Besides their widespread availability, certain qualities of judicial positions are outstanding. Some of these traits, such as salary and length of tenure, can be specified, and Table 3-1 compares judicial salaries and office tenures with those of legislators and certain administrative offices.

Historically, salaries of state legislators have often been downgraded, and a more relevant comparison is between judges' salaries and those of major administrative officials. The salaries of both trial and appellate judges compare favorably with those of major administrators and only top executives in the states receive higher salaries than judges.

Another desirable feature of judicial positions is the long term of office, granting security and freeing incumbents from some of the cares of campaigning. Appellate judicial terms are quite long, and even trial courts average longer terms than the majority of other state offices. Sixteen states allow appellate judges from 10 to 21 years in office, and at the other extreme only 14 states have terms as short as four years for trial court judges. Four states, Massachusetts, New Hampshire, New Jersey, and Rhode Island, have lifelong tenure for all judges during good behavior.

[1] *Book of the States, 1970–71* (Lexington, Ky.: Council of State Governments, 1970), p. 121.
[2] *Book of the States, 1970–71,* pp. 117–19.

TABLE 3-1   COMPARISON OF MEAN SALARY LEVELS
              AND TENURE RANGES OF LEGISLATIVE, JUDICIAL,
              AND SELECTED ADMINISTRATIVE POSITIONS, 1969

Position	Mean salary level	Tenure of office range
Member State Legislature (50 states)	$ 6,519	Two to four years
Major Trial Judge (50 states)	22,623	Four years to life tenure during good behavior (average: 6.7 years)
Appellate Court Judge (50 states)	24,201	Five years to life tenure during good behavior (average: 8.2 years)
Secretary of State (49 states)	19,334	Usually same as governor
Director of Highway Dept. (47 states)	23,178	Correlated with governor

Source: Book of the States, *1970-71 (Lexington, Ky.: Council of State Governments, 1970)*

The exceptional state is Vermont, which limits all judicial tenure to two years.

The quality of work involved in judicial duties is another desirable feature of judgeships. Judges have great scope for sustained and rigorous intellectual activity and occasions for creative and innovative work as well. It is not surprising that judicial posts rank very high in public esteem and usually lead other occupations in prestige.[3]

Finally, judicial positions are desirable for the opportunities they present for exercise of political power and an impact on policy making. This feature of judgeships is implicit in much thinking about judicial selection systems and occasionally enters into campaigns for the selection of judges. For example, during the first half of the nineteenth century, Jacksonian Democrats condemned the courts as protectors of the rich after some state judges had decided cases upholding large interest rates and foreclosure procedures.[4] In an attempt to change the policy orientations of judges, some state legislatures converted appointive judgeships into elective ones and shortened judicial terms of office. Through changes in the recruitment system, the Jacksonians aimed to elect judges sympathetic to popular points of view and to exclude conservative judges. Missouri plan selection systems (explained below) also represent an attempt to exclude judges with certain political orientations. By making judges appointive rather than elective and bringing in a nonpartisan nominating commission, certain advocates try to exclude the same kinds of influences that the Jacksonians were so anxious to bring into the courts.[5]

Because judgeships fulfill especially important patronage functions, they

3 Bancroft C. Henderson and T.C. Sinclair, *Judicial Selection in Texas: An Exploratory Study* (Houston, Texas: University of Houston Public Affairs Research Center, 1965), p. 87, as an example.
4 William Carpenter, *Judicial Tenure in the United States* (New Haven: Yale University Press, 1918), pp. 172–73.
5 Richard A. Watson and Rondal G. Downing, *The Politics of the Bench and the Bar* (New York: John Wiley & Sons, Inc., 1969), Chap. 1.

provide "much of the fuel for party engines,"[6] particularly for party workers who aspire to high level rewards. For the large number of lawyers active in state politics, a court post may represent the supreme attainment of a successful legal career. Minority group participants in state politics view a judgeship, with its high social and professional prestige, as an especially desirable goal. Unlike some administrative areas of state government, the number of judicial positions has not been reduced by civil service or administrative reorganization.

Although parties are concerned mainly with the patronage aspects of judgeships, other groups have different motivations. Bar associations, for example, are vitally concerned with judges' attitudes toward the handling of cases, and only minimally interested in the patronage aspects. Because the daily routines and success of lawyers are determined in part by the treatment they receive in court, they are much concerned with judges' professional behavior and attitudes toward litigation. Governors and legislators, on the other hand, use judicial appointments to reward friends and close associates in state politics. Depending on the nature of their linkages to the courts, different groups have different motivations in recruitment and set up varying criteria for the selection of judges. These different group motivations account in part for the state variations in selection systems.

SELECTION SYSTEMS

There are presently five different selection systems in use by the states. They are:

1. Gubernatorial appointment. The power of selection is exercised directly by the governor, using patronage, professional, or other considerations.

2. Legislative election. The choice is made by vote of the legislature on the basis of gubernatorial influence, patronage, or other factors.

3. Nonpartisan election. Judges are chosen in elections that formally exclude political parties from participation. Informal influences from political leaders or bar organizations may influence the election results.

4. Partisan election. The choice of judges is made in elections that admit political parties to participate. Party primaries are normally part of the election procedure.

5. Missouri plan. This is the most complex selection system and has three essential parts. First, slates of candidates are chosen by a nominating commission appointed by the governor. The governor then selects a judge from the list of names submitted by the commission. Finally, voters review the appointment by means of a referendum in which the judge runs unopposed on his record.

The distribution of selection systems among the states is shown in Table 3-2.

Although the elective methods of selection are favored over others, no single system predominates. Partisan and nonpartisan election methods are used in twenty-seven states, and the Missouri plan is popular with ten adherents. The more traditional methods are the least popular: seven states

---

[6] Wallace S. Sayre and Herbert Kaufman, *Governing New York City* (New York: Russell Sage Foundation, 1960), p. 538 and Chap. 15 generally.

TABLE 3–2   METHODS OF JUDICIAL SELECTION IN THE STATES
(Appellate and Major Trial Courts)

Partisan election (N = 17)	Election by legislature (N = 5)	Appointment (N = 7)	Missouri plan (N = 10)	Nonpartisan election (N = 15)
Much party influence and little bar influence			Little party influence and much bar influence	
Alabama	Connecticutª	Delaware	Alaska	Arizona
Arkansas	Rhode Island	Hawaii	California	Californiaᵇ
Florida	South Carolina	Maine	Colorado	Idaho
Georgia	Vermont	Maryland	Illinois	Michigan
Indiana	Virginia	Massachusetts	Iowa	Minnesota
Kansas		New Hampshire	Kansas	Montana
Kentucky		New Jersey	Missouri	Nevada
Louisiana			Nebraska	North Dakota
Mississippi			Oklahoma	Ohio
Missouri			Utah	Oregon
New Mexico				South Dakota
New York				Tennessee
North Carolina				Washington
Oklahoma				Wisconsin
Pennsylvania				Wyoming
Texas				
West Virginia				

ªFormally legislature, actually by nomination of governor.
ᵇSome states are listed under more than one heading because they select judges of different courts by different methods.
Source: State Court Systems (*Lexington, Ky.: Council of State Governments, 1970*), The Extent of Adoption of the Non-Partisan Appointive Elective Plan for the Selection of Judges (*Chicago: American Judicature Society, 1969*).

use gubernatorial appointment, while only five choose judges by legislative election. Several states, such as California and Missouri, use different methods for selecting different judges.

State recruitment plans have tended to follow fashion by responding to popular ideas at different historical periods, particularly in adoption of the initial method. Many states have not varied from the selection system adopted at their admission into the union. For example, the original thirteen states began either with gubernatorial appointment, the method continued from colonial experience, or legislative election, the method favored by some states immediately after the Revolution. Ten of the thirteen states have retained one of the two traditional methods, and only New York, North Carolina, and Pennsylvania switched to partisan elections during the Jacksonian pressure for popular reforms. Among those states that recruit by partisan elections, eastern and southern states, the areas that were most affected by the Jacksonian movement, predominate. On the other hand, western and midwestern states, sections that were most affected by the progressive and nonpartisan movements at their admission to the union or shortly thereafter, account for most of the nonpartisan adherents.

Although there have been various minor changes in recruitment methods, the major contemporary pattern of change has been toward adoption of the Missouri-type plan. It usually is featured as a "reform" of judicial

TABLE 3–3   INITIAL ADOPTION AND CHANGE OF JUDICIAL
SELECTION SYSTEMS IN THE AMERICAN
STATES BY HISTORICAL PERIODS

Method of selection	Period			
	1776–1831	1832–1885	1886–1933	1934–1968
By legislature	48.5	6.7	0.0	0.0
Gubernatorial appointment	42.4	20.0	10.7	5.6
Partisan election	9.1	73.3	25.0	11.1
Nonpartisan election	—	—	64.3	11.1
Missouri plan	—	—	—	72.2
	100.0	100.0	100.0	100.0

Source: Charles Haynes, The Selection and Tenure of Judges, *National Conference of Judicial Councils, 1944;* Journal of the American Judicature Society, *various volumes.*

selection rather than a mere "change." By 1940 it was adopted by Missouri and California and since 1956, eight additional states have adopted the plan. The strength of the movement toward the Missouri-type plan can be gauged by the fact that during the past twenty-five years no state has changed to any method other than the Missouri plan. Hawaii is really not an exception since, at admission to the union, that state simply continued the appointive plan that had been followed during territorial status.

A complete picture of the relation of changes in judicial recruitment to historical periods is pictured in Table 3-3. Included are all instances in which a court changed the method of selection. Some of the changes represented modifications for a single court or several courts rather than changes in the entire court system.

In each period represented there are dominant preferences expressed for different selection methods. The period of early statehood favored either continuation of appointive procedures used in the colonies or, in postrevolution states, the innovation of election by the state legislature. Later, the Jacksonian democratic movement, with its emphasis on participation through partisan involvement, and the nonpartisan progressive movement, which distrusted partisan involvements, dominated modifications in judicial selection during their respective periods of popularity. In the most recent period the Missouri-type plan has clearly outdistanced other plans in frequency of adoption.

Like the popularity of the partisan and nonpartisan election plans during certain periods, adoption of the Missouri system is a response to contemporary social developments. Of particular importance is the twentieth century professionalization of the law. Development of formal legal education and strong lawyers' organizations have strengthened the pressures for adequate "legal" qualifications in the judiciary. In a typical state the campaign for the Missouri plan has been led by legal groups, often with the opposition of local parties.[7] The assumption in the movement is that the governor, choosing from a panel nominated by a commission with legal

7 For an account of the adoption of the Missouri plan, see Jack W. Peltason, "The Missouri Plan for the Selection of Judges," *The University of Missouri Studies,* 20, 1945.

representation, will more likely select candidates who have superior legal qualifications.

PROCESSES OF JUDICIAL SELECTION

The structures of selection systems do not necessarily indicate how judges are chosen in actual practice. Selection systems consist of a set of formal rules and prescriptions; additional practices emerge in the implementation of selection. Indeed, inspection of the actual process of judicial recruitment in the states reveals not only that important behaviors are added to selection procedures, but that the actual process of selection may in some respects contradict the formal provisions for selection.

Partisan and nonpartisan elections

A characteristic of judicial recruitment in these states is that many judges are not initially elected, but are appointed. In an analysis of the period 1948–1957 for elective states, James Herndon found that of 434 Supreme Court justices who first attained office, 242 or 55.8 per cent entered office by appointment.[8]

This rather discrepant method of selection in an elective system is possible through the governor's power of interim appointment, which works in this manner: Apparently acting in conformity with a general understanding, many judges will resign or retire a short time before the end of their terms. This creates a vacancy which the governor has the power to fill by appointment to the unexpired term. These interim appointments often become permanent selections because of the great success judicial incumbents usually have in elections. In one study of subsequent elections involving such appointees in Wisconsin, more than one-third were not contested; in those contested, fewer than ten percent of the appointed judges were defeated.[9]

Where nonpartisan elections are used, partisan influences are nonetheless often present in the process of selection. For example, about half of the judges in nonpartisan states list some form of party affiliation in official biographies. Party organizations, under nonpartisan disguises, often play an active part in the campaigns.[10] This is the case in Minnesota, where judges have run as a bloc and political parties have endorsed them, thus making their partisan affiliations easily visible. In Michigan, a nonpartisan state, judges are openly nominated at party conventions and then supported by party organizations in ensuing campaigns.[11]

8 James Herndon, "Appointment as a Means of Initial Accession to Elective State Courts of Last Resort," *North Dakota Law Review,* 38 (1962), 60–73.
9 Jack Ladinsky and Alan Silver, "Popular Democracy and Judicial Independence," *Wisconsin Law Review* (1966), 132–33, n. 14.
10 Herbert Jacob, *Justice in America* (Boston: Little, Brown and Company, 1965), p. 98.
11 Malcolm Moos, "Judicial Elections and Partisan Endorsements of Judicial Candidates in Minnesota," *American Political Science Review,* 35 (1941), 69–75; Sidney Ulmer, "The Political Party Variable on the Michigan Supreme Court," *Journal of Public Law,* 11 (1962), 352–62.

In partisan elections of the judiciary we might expect more competition, more vigorous activity, and more intense partisanship, but judicial elections seldom live up to these expectations. Although judicial offices are generally contested at the same elections and appear on the same ballots as other offices, judicial contests are generally characterized by low turnouts, casual campaigns, and voter acquiescence. There is a more pronounced tendency than in other elections not to contest incumbent officeholders and, if there are contests, for the incumbents to win. For example, in Louisiana between 1945 and 1960 there were seven defeats out of 304 elections involving 169 different judges for district and appellate courts. In the same state were 26 judges who had served a period of time covering three elections. Of these, three had never faced opposition, sixteen faced opposition in only one election, five in two elections, and only two had been opposed in all three elections.[12]

Inactive as most judicial elections are, occasional active judicial elections are apt to occur under partisan systems. Experience indicates that it is all but impossible to arouse voters in judicial contests in nonpartisan elections, even when the seemingly explosive questions of judges' handling of sex and communism issues are introduced into the campaign.[13] On the other hand, Louisiana politics furnishes examples of heated contests for judicial office, including a number of elections for the Supreme Court. The most colorful incident is provided by Chief Justice Fournet's career. Justice Fournet originally secured his office in 1934 through Huey Long's manipulation of the election. Judge Pony, an opponent of Long and Fournet, referred to the court decision which validated Long's stratagem in these terms: "[The judges who ordered a new primary] are stool pigeons of that lying scoundrel, Huey P. Long, who has forfeited his right to live" and have "disgraced the court. In my opinion they have put themselves in the class of hog thieves."[14] Two terms and 28 years later, Chief Justice Fournet again faced formidable opposition in the Democratic primary. James Nelson Lee, his chief opponent, attacked Fournet's honesty and business dealing while on the court, while Fournet accused Lee of circulating a "lie-laden sheet" and acting "below the dignity of any man who seeks the important office of supreme court justice."[15] The vote in both primaries was extremely close, and the campaign was bitterly fought to the end. The vote was:

First primary		Runoff primary	
Fournet	47.6%	Fournet	51.5%
Lee	46.3	Lee	48.5
Thompson	6.1		

Fournet's career is an example of partisan politics for judicial selection in Louisiana. Other states have also had instances of partisan factionalism in judicial elections.

12 Kenneth N. Vines, "The Selection of Judges in Louisiana," *Tulane Studies in Political Science,* 8 (1962), 114–16.
13 Ladinsky and Silver, "Popular Democracy," 147–62.
14 *The New Orleans Times-Picayune,* 9 August 1934, p. 1.
15 *The New Orleans Times-Picayune,* 30 August 1962, Section II, p. 2.

Gubernatorial appointment

Most state appointive systems are much like the presidential system of appointment of federal judges, except that there is little equivalent to senatorial courtesy on the state level. More important are the background of the judge, the political needs and strategies of the governor, and the roles of such groups as the state bar association and political party factions. Many of the governor's appointees to judicial office have previously served in the legislature where they can establish reputations as party supporters and thus tempt the governor to reward them with judicial positions for their past loyalty and service to the party. At other times the governor may appoint a candidate from a particular section of a state in order to bolster his influence in a geographical area where his party's prospects are weak.[16]

One careful study of a gubernatorial appointment in a western state has analyzed the campaign undertaken by a candidate for the appointment.[17] The campaign was as carefully planned and energetically carried out as campaigns for elective office. Attention was concentrated on the mobilization of important political groups of several kinds. Private groups such as labor and public utility firms were enlisted, ethnic and minority groups normally found in the governor's party were mobilized, and local party organizations were brought into service. Finally, an effort was made to secure the support of a variety of law firms and sitting judges in order to project the image of a legally qualified nonpartisan aspirant. Despite his energetic campaign, the candidate failed to get the appointment.

A governor can make an appointment which serves a variety of purposes. He can make the appointment in order to gain immediate political advantage or to reward specifically for past services, or he can appoint someone who stands out primarily because of legal reputation and endorsement of legal groups. Governors in the appointive states make their appointments according to political needs and the governor's conception of his role as recruiter. One governor was described as making appointments that "invariably . . . have had a . . . readily apparent connection to a gubernatorial strategy for election and re-election."[18]

Missouri-type plans

Legal reformers, pressing for adoption of this method of recruitment, frequently say that its operation will take judicial selection "out of politics." Few could be so naive as to believe that the selection of judges could be nonpolitical in nature. What is meant presumably is that the Missouri-type selection would take selection out of *partisan* politics. A thorough study of the operation of the Missouri plan in Missouri indicates that not only has judicial selection there evolved a political pattern of its own, but also

---

[16] Jacob, *Justice in America,* pp. 96–99.
[17] John E. Crow, "Subterranean Politics: A Judge is Chosen," *Journal of Public Law,* 12 (1963), 275–89.
[18] Ibid., p. 288.

that the recruitment of judges has been linked in important ways to Missouri politics in general.[19]

One of the most interesting features of the plan is the great influence of the judiciary in selecting their own colleagues. Each of the three Missouri commissions, which nominate judges for different courts, consists of a combination of laymen, lawyers, and a sitting judge who presides over the commission. The lawyers are elected by all the attorneys in the court's district, the lay members are appointed by the governor, and the judge is the presiding judge of the courts of appeals of that area. Because he has a greater stake in the nomination of judicial colleagues than do the other members of the commission, the presiding judge ordinarily works devotedly and with much energy. Moreover, his influence with the other commission members is great because he has common professional ties with the lawyers and deference and respect from the laymen. In addition, the judge has an appreciation of the political perspective of the governor, since his own appointment was an outcome of that aspect of the political world. For these reasons the judge was rated as the most effective influence on the commission in forming politically influential combinations.

The lawyer members of the commission were less influential than is generally assumed to be the case under this selection plan. They not only tended to defer to the presiding judge, but their influence was weakened by divisive interests. The assumption that all lawyers agree on such questions as judicial appointments and do not have divergent perspectives is a common mistake. In fact, lawyers tend to be polarized around two general orientations, that of the plaintiff lawyers who represent and identify with injured persons in personal injury cases, and that of the defendant lawyers who have as clients the parties being sued, such as insurance companies and other business concerns. Plaintiff lawyers and defendant lawyers usually have separate bar associations, and in Missouri each association fielded its own slate of candidates for membership on the commission. Once on the commission, the lawyers were divided in their interpretations of the desirability of the candidates. Because of these differences, lawyer members of the nominating commissions rarely were able to form a united front and this minimized their influence.

But the influence of lay commission members was weakest of all, despite the implicit assumption in the Missouri plan that they would represent the public interest. Because of their lack of familiarity with and general awe of the technicalities of the law, the lay members have turned to the judge on the commission for direction. Their most positive contribution has been representation of the governor's perspective. On occasion, lay members have conveyed direct statements from a governor, but more generally they convey the governor's point of view because of their general awareness and experience with personalities and problems in his political life, and how judicial appointments might affect them.

---

[19] The following discussion of the operation of the Missouri plan is taken from Richard A. Watson and Rondal G. Downing, *The Politics of the Bench and the Bar: Judicial Selection Under the Missouri Nonpartisan Court Plan* (New York: John Wiley & Sons, Inc., 1969), especially Chaps. 1 and 10.

The influence of the governor has been exceptionally strong in Missouri plan operations. Indeed, the most realistic assessment of the Missouri operation is that it embodies a process of gubernatorial selection, and that the perspective of the bar, the judiciary, and the public expressed through the commission simply sets the outer limits of the governor's influence. This study of the Missouri plan operation in Missouri concludes that governors "have used their appointments to reward friends or past political supporters" and have implemented the plan very largely from a personal and political standpoint.[20]

One of the most important effects of the operation of the plan has been its institution of life tenure for judges in Missouri. The plan formally provides for electoral review of judges after one year's service on the bench, and the judge runs unopposed on his record. In theory this referendum is supposed to provide for public review of appointed judges. In practice the reviews have been virtually without effect, since in only one of 179 elections held under the plan has a judge been turned down—and that under extraordinary circumstances. Because of general public timidity and un-awareness of judical issues, the elections provide no protection for the public. The safe tenures of Missouri plan appointees are in marked contrast to preplan conditions, when both circuit and appellate judges met with frequent defeats, particularly in general elections.

IMPACT OF DIFFERENT SELECTION SYSTEMS

Efforts directed toward judicial recruitment have led to much activity in state politics. Although most of the effort has probably been inspired by thoughts of the reward, profit, and patronage of judicial positions, there has been some concern with the character of judges likely to be produced by certain selection systems. Such concerns have most often been expressed by Missouri plan advocates, sure that their plan recruits judges with superior qualifications. But does it? Are there any differences between judges selected according to the Missouri plan and those selected according to other methods?

Herbert Jacob has systematically investigated and compared the charac-teristics of judges chosen under the five different selection systems.[21] He finds that judges chosen under the different methods do differ, but not always as we might expect. For example, judges chosen by the Missouri plan do not have notably better legal education than judges chosen under other plans, and Missouri plan judges are more localistic (educated and born in the vicinity of their court) than other judges. This is contrary to the picture of the Missouri plan judge as highly educated and cosmopolitan. In a specific investigation of judges from the state of Missouri, Watson and Downing also find that Missouri plan judges have rather minimal legal

---

20 Watson and Downing, *The Politics of the Bench and the Bar*, pp. 338–39.
21 Herbert Jacob, "The Effect of Institutional Differences in the Recruitment Process: The Case of State Judges," *Journal of Public Law*, 33 (1964), 104–19.

educations and tend to be associated with local factors rather than out-of-state or national experiences.[22] But they have had somewhat greater previous experience as judges than other groups. On the other hand, both those judges chosen by the state legislature and those elected under partisan systems have more frequently had political experience, such as legislative and law enforcement positions, than other groups of judges. This is precisely what we would expect, because of closer involvement of these selection plans with the institutions of state government and political parties. Jacob also finds that governors appoint an unusually large proportion of former legislators to judicial positions. As indicated earlier, we would expect that the governor's involvement with legislators in effectuating his state programs would lead to obligations and rewards payable via judicial appointments.

Although seldom fully articulated, selection plans imply some pattern of behavior of those chosen by the particular system. For example, legal advocates of the Missouri plan generally claim that those selected have greater objectivity and legal expertise, while partisan advocates claim that those elected by their system will be more sensitive to democratic impulses. Critics of the Missouri plan claim that judges so selected will be conservatively biased and act in terms of conformity.

The point is that the Missouri plan will not produce a maverick. On the other hand, if you select your judges under the elective system, you may get all kinds of wacky characters going on the bench, who will frequently dissent from the views of their colleagues, and who will air different viewpoints and thus let a little ventilation into the process of justice.[23]

But the detailed investigation of the Missouri plan in the state of Missouri reveals that attorneys in the state believe that Missouri plan judges are just as objective as those who were previously selected under a different method. The investigators were able to find no significant bias in the judicial behavior of judges chosen under the plan. Also, plan judges actually dissented more than had previous judges, and hence were less conforming in their decisions on the courts.

ATTRIBUTES OF JUDGES

As we have seen, the methods by which judges are selected do not adequately predict the character of these judges. At best the selection system provides a preliminary screening function tending to admit and exclude general types. There are reasons, however, for knowing more about the men who become judges, including what their backgrounds were and what kinds of experience they have had. Judgeships are among the highest rewards and most sought after patronage in state politics, and their disposition among political groups is important. Another reason for knowing about the

---

[22] Watson and Downing, *The Politics of the Bench and the Bar,* Chap. 6.
[23] Ibid., p. 319.

TABLE 3-4   SELECTED BACKGROUND
CHARACTERISTICS OF STATE SUPREME
COURT JUDGES, 1969

Characteristics	Percent of Judges (N = 306)
Spent childhood in same state as court	89.0
Spent childhood in same region but not state as court	6.1
Attended law school in same state as court	60.4
Attended law school in same region but not state as court	20.5
Had law degree	92.4
Held previous state or local judgeship	31.2
Held at least one nonjudicial political office	72.5

Source: Various volumes of Who's Who and other state publications.

personal characteristics of judges is that knowledge of these features can help us understand their activities. A number of studies of state courts have shown that the decisional and policy-making activities of judges are related to certain features of their social backgrounds and past political experiences.[24] Therefore, by knowing more about the judges themselves we can learn something about their political behavior in arriving at decisions and forming policies for the courts.

We have investigated the backgrounds and experiences of all state supreme court justices sitting in 1969 in order to learn something of their personal characteristics. Our data consisted of an analysis of the biographies of 306 supreme court judges. In addition to personal characteristics, we were interested in such factors as education, political party affiliation, and past political and legal experiences.

Based on Table 3-4, we can construct a profile consisting of a number of generalizations about the judges sitting on American state courts of last resort.

They have formal legal training

Fewer than 10 percent of the state judges sitting in 1969 did not have law degrees. Most states require that judges have some sort of legal training, but few specify that the training must involve a formal law degree. An occasional state, such as West Virginia, following the Jacksonian tradition, requires only that a judge be a qualified voter, fulfill certain residence requirements, and not have such disqualifications as being a pauper, felon, or having a conviction for treason. The Louisiana Constitution requires simply that judges be "learned in the law" and have practiced law within the state for a short time. Because of such loose requirements, it is still possible in some states to pass the bar examinations by means short of a formal law degree, such as serving an apprenticeship with a law firm, attending correspondence school or law institutes, or self-study. The late governor of

24 For example, see Stuart Nagel, "Political Party Affiliation and Judges' Decisions," *American Political Science Review*, 55 (1961), 843–51; Ulmer, "The Political Party Variable on the Michigan Supreme Court."

Louisiana, Huey Long, is said to have passed the state bar examination after a one year cram course. Although such practices are still possible, the more rigorous quality of state bar examinations and the professionalization of the law make them rare.

They are recruited and trained locally

Because of their association with the concept of representation, we expect state legislators to have stronger ties than do judges with the districts they serve. However, judges also can often be identified with particular local constituencies. Trial judges are usually appointed from particular districts, hold court within these districts, and service clienteles within their bounds. Although supreme court judges are usually selected from the state at large, they too, such as those in Louisiana, are sometimes selected in order to represent particular districts. Table 3-4 indicates the strong local features involved in the socialization and training of state supreme court judges. Only 11 percent did not grow up in the states they served as judges, and only 1 in 16 from a region other than the state of his court. Localism was also reflected in the legal training of these judges, for they usually attended law schools within their states, or at least within the region of their court.

Localistic influences in the recruitment of state judges should occasion little surprise. The selection of judges is, in any of the selection systems, tied in some manner to the political processes of state politics. In various ways the selection of state judges involves judges in the electoral process (as in partisan and nonpartisan elections), in executive politics (when gubernatorial appointments or the Missouri plan are used), and in the legislative process (when the choice of judges is by legislative selection). Electoral processes have deep roots in local influence, while gubernatorial appointments usually involve a close group of supporters and partisans; legislative politics in judicial selection, like legislative politics in general, has deep local roots.

In judicial politics, local political influences and locally focused legal training tend to go hand in hand, each supporting the other. Among the rationalizations cited for legal training at the local law school is the necessity of education in state legal concepts in order to pass the state bar examination. Also stressed is the gaining of familiarity with local law in order to attain skill in community practice. An important product of attendance at the state law school is association with future political activists, many of whom are utilizing the training and associations at the state university for entrance into local politics.

They have prior political experience

State judges attain their positions only after years of activity and occupancy of other political offices. As a group, the state judges in our study have held two or more (2.3 average) offices before gaining their judgeships. There is, however, no career route that is standard preparation for judges, and they have held a variety of posts ranging from national to state, administrative, and legislative office. More than half of the state judges have held some sort of state judicial posts, such as state's attorney or local district attorney, and one-third have held a state judgeship before their accession to the supreme court. The variety of political experiences represented in the careers of state judges indicates the many paths to the state judiciary. Whatever the path taken, the experiences gained are valuable resources in attaining election or appointment to the high status positions of the supreme court. The comparatively modest number of judges who reached their positions after previous service in other courts indicates that in-service promotion is not a strong feature of the political careers of supreme court judges. More important than movement through the court system is experience in the state political system. Occupancy of minor judicial positions involves a certain amount of insulation from the political system, and may not prepare the candidate for advancement.

POLITICAL PARTIES AND RECRUITMENT

Political parties play major roles in the selection of state officials. Their domination of the election process, their importance in gubernatorial politics, and their crucial part in legislative processes all indicate their importance in the selection of state officials. Formally, of course, the nonpartisan states exclude parties from judicial elections, but in practice these elections often become linked to parties in informal ways, as Moos and Ulmer have shown in studies of the nonpartisan election of judges in Minnesota and Michigan.

Despite much talk about "taking judicial selection out of politics," nearly all state judges are identifiably associated with a party. Either through past activities under party auspices, candidacy under a party label, or simple party identification, state judges are involved in the state partisan system. Given the importance of judgeships as political positions, we would be surprised if parties relinquished their interest in judicial recruitment. To test the extent of judicial partisan associations, we investigated the partisan backgrounds of all judges of state courts of last resort sitting in 1969. Of the 317 judges included, we were able to link all but 11 with a political party, based either on past associations or personal partisan identification.

The state supreme court judges divided 60.1 percent Democratic and 39.9 percent Republican. The partisan associations of judges reflected the nature of the party system within their states. That is, in one party states the judges were affiliated with the party that dominated; in states with more competitive party systems, the judges were more evenly divided between the two parties. The relationship between judges' party affiliations and the states' party system is demonstrated by Table 3-5, which compares legislative party affiliations with those of judges in several varieties of state party systems.

In general the partisan distribution of judges approximates that of lower house legislators. Such a general comparison provides convincing evidence that judges are linked to states' party systems. Where the parties do not compete evenly, as in one-party Democratic states and in modified one-

TABLE 3–5   COMPARISON OF JUDGES' AND LEGISLATORS'
(LOWER HOUSE) PARTY AFFILIATIONS IN
DIFFERENT STATE PARTY SYSTEMS (1969),
$N = 386$, $N = 5542$

Party system	Supreme court judges % Democratic	Lower house legislators % Democratic
One-party Democratic	100.0	94.9
Modified one-party Democratic	89.1	69.0
Two-party competitive	44.6	48.2
Modified one-party Republican	11.5	31.1

Source: Austin Ranney, "Parties in State Politics," in Politics in the American States: A Comparative Anaysis (2d ed.), ed. Herbert Jacob and Kenneth N. Vines (Boston: Little, Brown and Company, 1971), p. 87; The Book of the States, 1970–71; various record books of the states.

party Democratic and Republican states, judges tend to reflect the dominant party more strongly than legislators. Doubtless, governors in such dominant party states utilize their appointive powers to reward political actives from the dominant parties. Probably, governors rarely find good political reasons to appoint judges from weak parties in the states.

IV THE JUDICIAL ROLE

THEORY OF THE JUDICIAL ROLE

In Chapter I, we stressed the ways in which state courts are deeply involved in various aspects of state politics. At the same time, the courts themselves are distinctive political institutions because of the many formal legal rules surrounding them. For example, state courts sometimes seem to be the most formal of institutions: they are insulated to an important extent from partisan politics, they appear to make decisions according to legal traditions and rules, and their linkages to the public are severely restricted. At other times, however, courts and judges become involved in partisan politics through recruitment of party activists to important judicial positions and court pronouncements which have significant impact on public policy.

This combination of court characteristics sometimes makes it difficult to understand exactly which factors affect judicial behavior. It is frequently unclear, for example, where legal and political variables have the greatest impact on the courts, and how the two sets of variables relate to one another. One way of viewing the state courts, which may help to clarify various features of state judicial behavior, is through the concept of *role*. Role tells us how judges view their own actions under various circumstances and, for that reason, presents information concerning some of the factors which shape judicial institutions.

When we speak of an individual's role, we mean something more precise than our everyday usage of the word, which refers to such things as an individual's influence in a group decision, his participation in a social or political event, or the part he plays in a stage production. The concept of role does include some of these ideas, but it encompasses much more. As generally used in the social sciences, role refers to sets of normative expectations regarding the proper behavior and personal qualities of the occupants of specific social or political positions.[1] These expectations may be viewed as various individuals' standards or methods of evaluation concerning how a person who holds a particular position ought to act. Expectations which are important in affecting the performance of roles include those of the individual whose behavior is the subject of analysis (for example, a judge), and those of other individuals who occupy positions linked in various ways to the main actor (such as lawyers, the public, and political party leaders).[2]

The meaning of role may become clearer with a familiar illustration. Being a medical doctor involves sets of expectations held by the doctor and by people with whom he interacts. Specifically, the doctor relates to his patients, nurses, fellow doctors, and pharmacists. To each of them he acts in a way which is defined by the interaction of expectations about what constitutes proper behavior for a doctor. The patient may expect sympathetic and skillful medical treatment, but the doctor may or may not act in this way, according to his own expectations and his awareness of the patient's expectations. The doctor-nurse relationship, involving professional superior-subordinate interaction, requires different sorts of behavior. To describe each of these various relationships between a doctor and others describes the role of a doctor.

An important advantage of role in the analysis of state courts is that the expectations important for behavior may be derived from a variety of sources and may include formal, legal prescriptions of behavior as well as informal expectations. If both are present and affect various aspects of the behavior of judges, they may be considered important variables shaping court

1 An important study which surveys the various meanings of role theory and terminology is Bruce J. Biddle and Edwin J. Thomas, eds., *Role Theory* (New York: John Wiley & Sons, Inc., 1966), especially pp. 3–63. Another work which is very useful in clarifying and explaining role concepts and terms is Neal Gross, Ward S. Mason, and Alexander McEachern, *Explorations in Role Analysis: Studies of the School Superintendancy Role* (New York: John Wiley & Sons, Inc., 1958), especially Chap. 4. The terminology and concepts used here are drawn largely from this study and from John C. Wahlke, Heinz Eulau, William Buchanan, and Leroy C. Ferguson, *The Legislative System: Explorations In Legislative Behavior* (New York: John Wiley & Sons, Inc., 1962). For additional discussion of the roles of state judges, see Henry Robert Glick, *Supreme Courts in State Politics* (New York: Basic Books, Inc., Publishers, 1971).
2 The interaction of expectations which defines the role of position incumbents is stressed in Talcott Parsons and Edward A. Shils, eds., *Toward a General Theory of Action* (New York: Harper & Row, Publishers, 1962), pp. 19–20.

institutions.[3] Expectations may be found in state statutes, court rules, and codes of judicial ethics, as well as in the perceptions of judges and other political actors of the judicial position.

Although relationships among various individuals are important in shaping political roles, political actors are also affected by a variety of personal, political, and judicial systems variables. The interplay between some of these factors and a description of various aspects of the judicial role are presented in Figure 4-1. These relationships are very general, but they indicate the major classes of variables which may affect judicial role orientations and suggest some of the important political actors who interact with judges. (Role orientation refers to the stance or position which actors adopt regarding their behavior toward various other individuals.)

We shall not examine or suggest in detail how personal and political systems variables affect role orientations, for this would require extensive theory and data beyond the scope of this discussion. Nevertheless, Figure 4-1 permits us to view a judge from a personal perspective as one who has experienced a distinctive series of events during his lifetime, acquiring values and attitudes which, along with other variables, predispose him to act in certain ways as a judge. At the same time, judges are considered as actors within a particular political and judicial system with formal and informal rules and practices which also affect the structure of political institutions and the behavior of its members.

Several examples may help to clarify the expected effects of some of these variables. The political socialization of most Americans, for example, includes learning experiences causing them to hold certain fundamental values about the American political process. Besides a belief in the goodness of democracy and respect for its political institutions, most Americans also have views of how political officials—including judges—should act. A generalized and abstract belief in equality before the law and the value of impartial, objective "justice" are examples of prevalent views. Judges have also acquired these values, but they undergo an additional, distinctive socialization process as a result of their formal law school training. Besides providing an individual with fundamental skills which enable him to become a practicing attorney, the law school experience conveys a set of attitudes and values about the judicial process and certain ways of viewing the judiciary as a governmental institution. These values include a more explicit respect for law and legal procedure and convey a set of ideas about the qualities and expected behavior of a "good" judge. We should also note here that judges continue to be resocialized once they become members of a court. They may be influenced by others to conform to court traditions and informal judicial practices, and may also try to reduce the influence of their personal attitudes and previous political experience in order to be more "objective" in their decision making.

Despite the resocialization, judges are also affected by their political attitudes, background characteristics, and psychological needs. We would hypothesize that the effects of early family life, which play a major part in

---

[3] On this point, see Wahlke et al., *The Legislative System*, pp. 9–10.

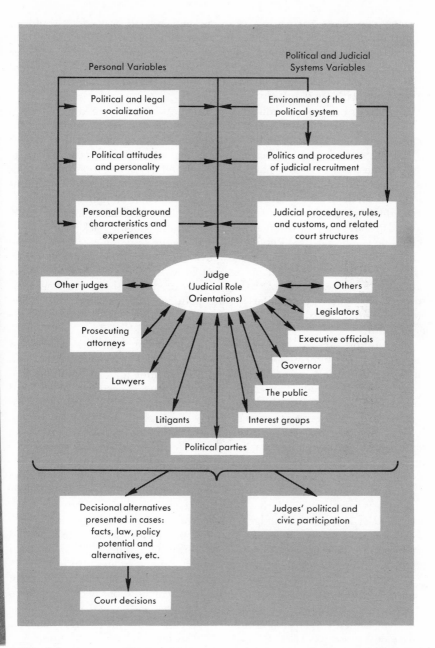

Personal Variables

Political and Judicial
Systems Variables

Political and legal
socialization

Environment of the
political system

Political attitudes
and personality

Politics and procedures
of judicial recruitment

Personal background
characteristics and
experiences

Judicial procedures, rules,
and customs, and related
court structures

Other judges

Judge
(Judicial Role
Orientations)

Others

Legislators

Prosecuting
attorneys

Executive officials

Lawyers

Governor

The public

Litigants

Interest groups

Political parties

Decisional alternatives
presented in cases:
facts, law, policy
potential and
alternatives, etc.

Judges' political and
civic participation

Court decisions

FIG. 4-1 Variables affecting judicial role orientations and a description of judges' role relationships.

shaping everyone's personality structure and related attitudes, would be important in predisposing a judge to adopt a distinctive role of orientation. For example, a severe or stern judge, or one concerned primarily with the intricate details of law and procedure, may have a personality different from a judge who is less severe and less interested in achieving strict compliance with legal rules.[4]

As Figure 4-1 shows, judicial role orientations also are affected by a variety of political systems factors. Aspects of the environment of the political system (which includes level of political party competition, degree of urbanism, and general socioeconomic character of the state) relate to one another, but may also have an indirect effect on the role orientations of judges. For example, the interactions among urbanism, party organization, and methods of recruitment may favor selection of judicial candidates from different parts of the state who also have different political backgrounds. Some may have an urban, Democratic, liberal background while others may reflect rural, Republican, and conservative views. Some judges may have an extensive history of active participation in politics; others may have held few political offices and have worked very little for party organizations. These kinds of variations may predispose judges to view their roles in different ways. Similarly, state political cultures vary, and judges from the urban northeast may be expected to differ from judges in the deep south.

In addition to the state political environment and the politics of recruitment, the judicial role is affected by judicial procedures, rules, and customs. Formal features of the judicial process limit judicial discretion and court jurisdiction, but trial and appellate court procedures, rules, and customs also provide a general framework and a set of basic guidelines for a variety of relationships among judges themselves and among judges, lawyers, litigants, and others involved in the functioning of the court. In some states, for example, appellate judges exercise a general supervisory function over the entire state court system in addition to their powers of appellate review. This power requires judges to adopt a role orientation toward the lower courts concerning the intensity of the exercise of their supervisory function. Similarly, judges on collegial appellate courts (those composed of a number of judges) must work as a group in order to reach a decision that reflects at least a majority point of view. Role orientations are important here because they help to clarify the ground rules or informal norms governing negotiations and discussions among judges on the court.

In addition to various factors which may affect judicial role orientations, Figure 4-1 presents a number of other political positions which relate to judges. As stated before, the interactions between judges and various actors linked to the courts are important because they affect the expectations of judges and others concerning proper judicial behavior and attributes.

Figure 4-1 does not differentiate among specific judicial positions, but it should be made clear that certain political relationships are more important for certain judicial positions than for others, and that the character of the

[4] For further discussion of this view, see Glendon Schubert, *The Judicial Mind* (Evanston, Ill.: Northwestern University Press, 1965), pp. 12–13.

relationships will differ among judges. The basic structure of court institutions and court rules of procedure and jurisdiction vitally affect the kinds of cases judges decide, the clientele who use the courts, and related judicial personnel who participate in litigation. In addition, actors in the state political system have different stakes in the outcomes of litigation in the various courts and impose different political obligations on judges at various levels of the judicial system. These kinds of variations are important in determining the specific character of state judicial roles.

The role of trial court judges, for example, differs in important ways from that of state appellate court judges. Several of the differences are evident in decision-making procedures and in relationships between judges. Trial court judges decide cases by themselves; they do not interact with other judges on the court through discussion, bargaining, persuasion, or voting in order to reach a decision. However, appellate review is one of the circumstances in which mutual interchange of role expectations is important in shaping the behavior of both trial and appellate court judges. An important question, for example, concerns how trial and appellate judges view each other's powers and authority, and the effects which appellate review has on the decisions and other actions of trial judges. Trial court judges may also interact with other trial judges at conferences called to consider proposals for court reorganization or changes in rules of procedure. At these times, trial court judges with interests in common concerning the operation of their courts may act together to oppose major alterations of the judiciary.

Decision making on appellate courts is quite different from that on the trial courts, and involves behavior which contributes to the distinctive political role. Many features of appellate court decision making can be examined from the perspective of role. Because they must interact on a continuing basis with their colleagues in reaching decisions and maintaining routine court operations, we can inquire into the attributes which judges believe members of the court should possess in order to be respected by the other judges. In addition, informal rules adopted by the court which are designed to maintain congenial personal relations also contribute to a description of interactions which define this aspect of the judicial role. Another important concern in a study of the role of appellate judges deals with relations among judges which directly involve the decision-making process. Since state courts are political institutions with the opportunity to make policy decisions, we must investigate the procedures and expectations which influence decision making. Questions concerning decision making include: What procedures are followed in the process of making decisions? How do judges respond to the ideas and suggestions of their colleagues? Are judges willing to negotiate and compromise their differences in order to reach decisions, or do they prefer formal discussion and voting? What factors relate to these different orientations? Do factions exist on the court, and what are the informal rules which govern dissenting and concurring opinions? What factors contribute to personal influence on the court? These questions deal with fundamental aspects of group relationships on appellate courts, and thus contribute to a description of the interactions among judges which constitute a major part of the judicial role.

Judges at different levels of the judicial hierarchy also have various kinds of relationships with litigants and judicial and law enforcement personnel. State supreme court judges may feel more isolated from other actors than trial judges because they have no court contacts with litigants, police officers, witnesses, and jurors. Since appellate courts deal only with the record established in the trial court, appellate judges interact only with attorneys during oral argument, when they may question them about aspects of their legal brief. This is the only direct contact they have with other major participants in court proceedings. Most of their time is devoted to research and writing in their own offices, and to conferences with their colleagues.

Trial and appellate judges also have different sorts of contacts with political parties, interest groups, the public, and other political officials. For several reasons trial judges are apt to have more intricate and long-lasting bonds to partisan, civic, and social groups. First, they are recruited to their court from the community in which the court is located. Prior to recruitment they had probably been somewhat active in local politics, and will remain familiar with local political groups. Most of their litigation also concerns individuals and businesses located in the community. In contrast, supreme court judges leave their community to sit on a court in another city and are less likely to remain closely attached to local political and social organizations.

Trial judges also are likely to remain more closely linked to local political groups because they generally serve for shorter terms than appellate court judges and must run for reelection more frequently. They need the continued support of political parties and interest groups in their campaigns.[5] Trial judges are also affected differently because they are more likely than supreme court judges to face opposition in their reelection campaigns. In contrast, the prestige of the supreme court seems to deter individuals from challenging the incumbent judge. The sitting judge principle—the idea that the incumbent ought to be retained in office when he runs for reelection—is more important for state supreme courts than for trial courts.[6] This does not mean that supreme court judges have no important relationships with groups outside of court, but it does suggest that the character of their role differs from that of trial court judges.

Our model of the judicial role includes two general sets of behavior which are affected by role orientations: court decision making and other forms of off-the-bench activity (such as participation in political party affairs and elections, participation in civic events, and membership in civic and social organizations). Certain features of these relationships need to be explained. Note that role orientations, personal variables, and political and judicial systems are not expected to provide a complete explanation for judicial decision making. These factors are related to variations in judicial decision

5 A useful discussion of the relationships between trial judges and political parties is found in Wallace S. Sayre and Herbert Kaufman, Governing New York City (New York: Russell Sage Foundation, 1960), Chap. 14.
6 Herbert Jacob, "The Effect of Institutional Differences in the Recruitment Process: The Case of State Judges," Journal of Public Law, 13 (1964), 116.

making, but consideration of them alone leads to an oversimplification of the decision-making process. Judges must make decisions within the limitations imposed by the facts and the law in the case. They are also limited by the dimensions of the issues and policy alternatives presented to them. An adequate explanation of decision making therefore needs to give attention to the particular circumstances involved in individual cases.

We have differentiated in Figure 4-1 between decision-making behavior and nondecisional behavior because different role orientations are related to each of these behavioral sets. For example, judges' interactions with their colleagues on an appellate court would be crucial in determining how they go about producing decisions. Similarly, relationships between trial judges and other court personnel would be important in affecting the way they conduct a trial. Expectations which are important in these relationships are different from those which determine whether judges will feel free to participate in party activities and other public events.

THE JUDICIAL ROLE IN STATE SUPREME COURTS

As our discussion of the theory of the judicial role has indicated, role analysis can help to clarify some of the fundamental norms and patterns of behavior which characterize judicial institutions. Several important questions about the judicial role concern the basic functions which courts fulfill in the state political system and the importance of judicial ethics in affecting a judge's off-the-bench behavior. We shall discuss both of these as they pertain to state supreme courts.

In order to investigate the state supreme court judicial role, we have gathered information on the role perceptions of supreme court judges in four states (Louisiana, Pennsylvania, New Jersey, and Massachusetts). Judges' perceptions of their role (how judges themselves view their job and their relationships with other political actors) were gathered through personal interviews with twenty-six of the twenty-eight members of the four courts.

The work of state supreme courts

The basic concern of judges is to settle conflicts presented to them in the form of court cases. Adhering to numerous formal procedures and customs, they hear the arguments of attorneys, engage in legal research and writing, and decide whether the decisions of lower courts should be upheld or reversed. In the course of performing these fundamental functions certain judges may also seek to accomplish various additional objectives. Appellate court judges, for example, may strive to formulate significant state policy in their decisions, or may supervise the actions of the trial courts. Others may not perceive the potential of the courts to perform these additional functions. Understanding how judges perceive this aspect of the judicial role is important, because courts may operate differently depending in part upon how judges view their functions in the political system. In addition, this aspect of the supreme court judicial role includes information relating to a description of important features of judicial institutions.

As part of our research on the judicial role, the judges were asked to describe how they viewed the job of a supreme court judge. They referred to five distinct orientations toward the functions which courts perform: (1) the ritualist; (2) the adjudicator; (3) the lawmaker; (4) the administrator; and (5) the constitutional defender. We shall describe each of these briefly.

Ritualist. Numerous features of the judicial process require routine performance of certain acts on a continuing, day-to-day basis. Activities such as supervising secretaries and law clerks and engaging in legal research and writing are some of the tasks which judges repeat throughout a court session. Performance of these tasks also has an affective aspect: some judges enjoy their job and find the judicial post a welcome change from more hectic political offices; others feel that their judicial tasks are burdensome, tiring, and unpleasant.

Adjudicator. As in the carrying out of other routine duties, judges perform certain essential functions in order to decide cases. Included in their descriptions of their functions were such things as listening to the arguments of attorneys in court and discussing the case with their colleagues. Some viewed their post simply in terms of the necessity of deciding cases, while others described their appellate jurisdiction and emphasized that their duties included determining whether the lower courts should be upheld or reversed.

Lawmaker. Especially significant for the judicial role is the orientation which views judges as participants in state lawmaking. This orientation recognizes the importance of courts as political agencies, with opportunities to do much more than simply dispose of court cases: judges make decisions which have the potential of substantially altering the interpretation of state law and its application to numerous economic, social, and political relationships.

Administrator. Certain judges in the four states also included in their orientations an important administrative function. This orientation includes two forms of control which the state supreme courts may exercise over the lower courts. First, the supreme court can review the decisions of lower courts and indicate the proper course of action which the lower courts are to follow in deciding cases in the future. Second, the supreme court has the power to make rules regulating the procedures and personal conduct of lower court personnel and lawyers practicing in the state.

Constitutional defender. This orientation is closely linked to conservative political ideologies and includes a belief that judges serve as important guardians of the American form of government by protecting the Constitution against various political enemies.

The distribution of judges' orientations toward the work of the supreme court is presented in Table 4-1. It is clear that most of the judges in all

TABLE 4-1   JUDGES' ORIENTATIONS TOWARD THE WORK
             OF STATE SUPREME COURTS

Orientation	N.J.[a] $N = 7$[b]	Mass. $N = 6$	Penna. $N = 6$	La. $N = 7$	Total of Four States $N = 26$
Ritualist	42.9%	66.7%	83.3%	28.6%	53.8%
Adjudicator	42.9	33.3	16.7	85.7	46.2
Lawmaker	57.1	16.7	17.7	0.0	23.1
Administrator	28.6	0.0	16.7	0.0	11.5
Constitutional defender	0.0	0.0	0.0	14.3	3.8

[a] Percentages will not total 100 because certain judges perceived more then one goal.
[b] Percentages are used in these distributions even though the Ns are small, because percentages seem to convey more meaning to the reader.

four states viewed their role in terms of the ritualist orientation and adjucation which involves procedures essential for carrying out the courts' primary function—settlement of cases at the appellate court level. These findings are not surprising in view of the explicit functions which judges must perform daily. Such long-range objectives as lawmaking may be less salient because they are indirect and must be accomplished in the course of making court decisions. The administrator and constitutional defender orientations were also unimportant to most judges.

Although the ritualist and adjudicator orientations were most prevalent, there are several important variations among the four courts concerning emphasis on law or policy making and the formal function of adjudication. More judges in Louisiana than in any other state adhered to the adjudicator orientation, and the New Jersey judges clearly outnumber the others in the lawmaker category. These variations focus on the crucial question of whether judges should feel free to make policy in their decisions, or whether the courts should be restricted to the more formal role of merely interpreting and applying existing law in the decision of cases.

In order to investigate this aspect of judicial functions in more detail, the judges were asked to evaluate the distinction between lawmaking and law-interpreting, and to indicate which position they believed was the proper one for judges to take. The distribution of their responses is presented in Table 4-2. Slightly over half of the judges adopted the law-interpreter position. About one-fourth viewed themselves at lawmakers, and some

TABLE 4-2   DISTRIBUTION OF LAW-INTERPRETERS,
             LAWMAKERS, AND PRAGMATISTS

Orientation	N.J. $N = 7$	Mass.[b] $N = 6$	Penna. $N = 6$	La. $N = 7$	Total of Four States $N = 24$
Law-interpreter	14.3%	50.0%	66.7%	85.7%	53.8%
Lawmaker	57.1	16.7	0.0	14.7	23.1
Pragmatist	28.6	16.7	33.3	0.0	19.2
Unknown[a]	0.0	16.7	0.0	0.0	3.8
Total	100.0	100.1	100.0	100.0	99.9

[a] Not ascertainable from interview response.
[b] Certain percentages will not total 100 because of rounding.

adopted a third position, identified here as the pragmatist, which is a combination of both the law-interpreter and lawmaker orientations. Pragmatists are those who believe that some cases are settled more easily by applying existing policies or rules to the issues and conflicts. The pragmatic view can be considered as a midpoint in a continuum in which the lawmaker and law-interpreter positions are at opposite poles.

We saw in Table 4-1 that the New Jersey and Louisiana judges in particular adopted divergent orientations toward judicial functions. Similar differences between these two states are shown in Table 4-2. Only one New Jersey judge adopted the law-interpreter position; the other New Jersey judges were either lawmakers or pragmatists. In contrast, all but one Louisiana judge adhered to the law-interpreter view. The Massachusetts and Pennsylvania Supreme Courts are closest in orientation to the Louisiana court; however, the orientations of the individual Massachusetts and Pennsylvania judges are somewhat more mixed.

Some evidence suggests that the differences between the New Jersey and Louisiana Supreme Courts may be explained in part as a reflection of variations in state political and judical systems, and the associated political attitudes of the judges. This explanation is consistent with our model of the judicial role in Figure 4-1 and indicates how role orientations may be linked to the backgrounds of the judges and the political environment of the states.

The New Jersey Supreme Court functions within the context of a distinctive political and judicial tradition which has affected the state courts at least since 1947, when a new state constitution was adopted.[7] Under the leadership of Arthur T. Vanderbilt, a prominent national leader of court reform, many changes of the state courts were incorporated into the new constitution. Vanderbilt's goals included creation of a well-integrated state court system, with the supreme court performing a leadership function through its powers to make rules governing the entire state judiciary. In addition, Vanderbilt believed the state supreme court should be a very active institution and seek ways to make significant state policy. When he became the first chief justice of the newly formed supreme court, Vanderbilt led it toward becoming a more dynamic institution.[8]

Vanderbilt has had a lasting effect on the New Jersey Supreme Court in various ways. First, three of the current judges had been closely associated with him either in law practice, personal friendship, or the fight for court reform, and probably share many of his views. In addition, many of the opponents to Vanderbilt's proposals for court change were older members of the bar and bench and are probably no longer active in the state courts.[9] Thus the impetus furnished by Vanderbilt and continued by the supreme court may have developed into a state political tradition.

---

[7] Richard N. Baisden, *Charter for New Jersey: The New Jersey Constitutional Convention of 1947* (Trenton: Division of the State Library, Archives and History, New Jersey Department of Education, 1952), pp. 40–41.
[8] Sidney M. Wolinshy, "Arthur T. Vanderbilt: The Amending Hand" (Honors thesis, Princeton University, 1958), pp. 108–9.
[9] Baisden, *Charter for New Jersey*, pp. 45, 49.

Just as New Jersey state politics appears to have influenced judges' orientations in that state, it also appears that the perceptions of the Louisiana judges are related to dominant features of the state political system. As Tables 4-1 and 4-2 show, the Louisiana judges adhered more frequently to the formal adjudicator and law-interpreter orientations, which view the judicial role as limited to the obligation to decide cases and apply existing law to court decisions. A possible explanation is that the state's conservative political environment has affected the judges' orientations to their role. The relationship between conservative political attitudes and emphasis on adjudication and law-interpreting lies in their common focus on limiting the scope of governmental authority. These two orientations seek to restrict judges to the formal powers allocated to them in a strict reading of the Constitution. A link between conservative political attitudes and role orientations is also found in the presence of the constitutional defender orientation which was adopted by one of the Louisiana judges.

As our previous discussion has indicated, the judicial role varies for judges at different levels of the judicial hierarchy. Trial procedures differ substantially from appellate procedures, and judges interact with different participants in the course of coming to a conclusion in a case. The specific tasks which each performs also vary. In addition, the nature of appellate court cases differs from those at the trial level. A portion of the supreme court's workload is composed of cases which involve few important legal or political questions, and are therefore not likely to affect public policy. There is little doubt concerning the outcome of many of these cases. The statutes or judicial doctrine pertaining to them are clear, and the lower courts will probably not be reversed. Other cases decided by state appellate courts, however, involve controversial issues which generate substantial disagreement concerning their resolution. These kinds of cases provide the appellate courts with more frequent opportunities to make significant public policy. In addition, in states where the mandatory jurisdiction of the supreme court has been limited (i.e., where the kinds of cases which it is required by law to hear are limited to a few categories) and where the court's discretionary jurisdiction is wide (i.e., where it may decide for itself which cases it wants to decide in addition to its regular jurisdiction), the courts may deal primarily with cases which raise controversial issues or those which have a wider impact on various publics. Under these circumstances, the policy-making role of the supreme court may be significant.

In order to investigate variations in judicial roles, the judges on the four supreme courts were asked to describe how they viewed the differences between a supreme court and a trial court position. Our intention was to determine which features of various judicial roles the judges perceived as most distinctive and important. As Table 4-3 shows, the judges most frequently perceived differences in the processes of adjudication or the specific tasks (rituals) which judges must perform at different levels of the judicial hierarchy. As our earlier discussion has indicated, these aspects of the judicial role are most visible because they constitute the normal routines of judges in the four states. Several responses drawn from the interviews clearly illustrate some of these fundamental differences in role

TABLE 4–3   JUDICIAL FUNCTIONS
DISTINGUISHING SUPREME
COURTS FROM LOWER COURTS

Differences perceived	Total of four states[a]
Adjudication	65.4%
Tasks	57.7
Lawmaking	26.9
None	3.8

[a]Percentages will not total 100 because certain judges perceived more than one difference.

orientations. For example, two judges described the differences in adjudication and specific tasks this way:

There's a difference between a trial of facts and appellate work where there's a greater concentration on the legal aspects of the case. . . . You hear testimony on the trial level. There's a lot of research on the appellate level and there's no time limit involved in researching a case. You spend a lot more time on it and there's working at night.

At the trial level a judge decides by himself or with a jury. . . . A trial judge is always bound by the books. . . . The situation on the appellate court is more like Monday morning quarterbacking. You see whether the trial court committed any prejudicial error.

Differences in particular tasks also affect the kinds of interaction of judges with other participants in the judicial process:

The work of an appellate judge is vastly different from that of a trial judge. Trial judges are always in the midst of the people. An appellate judge never sees or hears the witnesses. Here we read and hear the oral arguments of the lawyers. I would say that 75 per cent of our work is office work—study and research. Frankly, I believe that up here we lose contact with the people.

In addition to this emphasis on differences in routine tasks and adjudication, it should be noted that about one-quarter of the judges stated that the supreme court has a much greater opportunity to make law or policy through its decisions. Significantly, the New Jersey judges were predominant in this category. Of the seven judges who mentioned the special lawmaking function of the supreme court, four were in New Jersey; only one judge from each of the other four states perceived this distinctive aspect of the supreme court role. The differences in the two judicial positions were made very clear by one New Jersey judge who stated:

The supreme court has the responsibility of molding the law. The trial court does not. They should apply the principles as pronounced by the upper court. Most of our law is composed of common law principles amassed through a constitution. The great bulk of state law is common law—a development of history in the hands of judges. Judges have to mold the law into their concept of justice.

Judicial ethics and off-the-bench activity

An often discussed aspect of the judicial role is that judges should consciously seek to be impartial in making decisions. This is generally assumed to mean that judges should evaluate the facts and law pertaining to the case and produce a decision free from any nonjudicial bias or pressure. To ensure impartiality, judges are expected to insulate themselves from potential extrajudicial influence. They are to avoid any personal contact with individuals or groups who have a stake in the case and, ideally, should also have separated themselves from civic, social, and political organizations and business activities in which they had an interest prior to becoming a judge. This is designed to prevent a conflict between a judge's personal interests and his obligations to decide cases fairly.

The value placed on impartiality is probably higher in judicial decision making than in any other political office, and the goal of insulation and independence is a particularly distinctive and significant feature of the judicial role. The importance of impartiality becomes especially clear when judges are accused of having business interests which may have influenced their decisions, or when they engage in financial activities which *appear* to violate the high ethical and moral standards which society sets for judges. An instance in which these expectations were crucial involved two justices of the Illinois Supreme Court. It was disclosed that Justices Ray I. Klingbeil and Roy I. Solfisburg (Chief Justice) had acquired stock in a Chicago bank while a case involving one of the organizers of the bank was pending before the court. Justice Klingbeil received $2500 worth of bank stock as a gift, and Justice Solfisburg had borrowed money to buy stock at a special reduced price. The supreme court, in a majority opinion written by Justice Klingbeil, upheld a lower court decision favorable to the bank executive. Both judges claimed that the acquisition of stock had had no effect on their decisions in the case, and they denied any violation of judicial ethics. Nevertheless, a state investigating committee urged the judges to resign in order to reestablish the public's confidence in the judiciary; both judges retired from the bench.[10]

Although there are pressures for judges to insulate themselves in order to guard against conflicts of interest, other expectations may interfere, leading judges to take part in certain civic or social events. This stems from the special character of a judicial post and the personal qualities frequently attributed to judges. Judges would seem to have special opportunities to become leaders in their community because of the prestige of their office and the deference they receive from others. In addition, the judiciary is replete with myths suggesting that judges possess special, desirable personal qualities (e.g., wisdom, integrity, fortitude, compassion). The support and guidance by judges of various public events, programs, and worthy institutions would be invited. Nevertheless, judges must take care to stay away from any activities which could affect their impartiality.

10 *The New York Times,* 15 July 1969, p. 23; 1 August 1969, p. 34; 3 August 1969, p. 66.

In order to investigate how the state supreme court judges viewed judicial participation in off-the-bench activities, they were asked five questions dealing with general civic participation and other specific forms of activity, including membership in civic organizations, participation in business affairs, becoming leaders in civic groups, and speaking out on public issues. A scale constructed from their answers to all five questions indicates their general orientation to the propriety of judicial participation in nonjudicial activities (Table 4-4).

The judges generally placed certain restrictions on judicial participation in nonjudicial affairs, but there is some variation among them concerning this issue. The New Jersey and Pennsylvania judges placed the greatest limitations on judicial participation, and the Louisiana judges were the most permissive. The Massachusetts judges occupy a middle ground. The specific activities which account for most of the differences in Table 4-4 are those dealing with participation in business affairs and leadership roles in civic organizations. On both of these items, the Louisiana judges differed markedly from the others and indicated a greater willingness to allow judges to participate in activities which most other judges considered not permissible.

It is significant that the judges disagreed on this aspect of their role. It also seems clear that judges in some states may participate more than others, and that some differences exist in the potential of judges for becom-

TABLE 4–4   **PROPRIETY OF JUDGES' PARTICIPATION IN NONJUDICIAL AFFAIRS[a]**

Level of Participation Permitted	N.J.	Mass.	Penna.	La.	Total of Four States
Much[b]	0.0%	16.7%	0.0%	28.6%	11.5%
Some	14.3	33.3	16.7	57.1	30.8
Very little	42.9	50.0	50.0	14.3	38.5
None	42.9	0.0	33.3	0.0	19.2
Total	100.0	100.0	100.0	100.0	100.0

[a]The questions used to construct this table include:
1. Now, what about civic participation? Can a judge in your position feel free to participate in public affairs?
2. What about retaining membership in civic organizations?
3. What about participation in business affairs?
4. How about leadership? Can a judge accept the duties and responsibilities of leadership in a civic organization?
5. What about speaking out on public issues? Can a judge speak his mind on these?

The scale was constructed by assigning a weight of one to the first two questions and a weight of two to questions 3, 4, and 5, since these three items referred to more extensive and controversial forms of participation. The judges' responses to each question were given a score ranging from 0 to 2: 0 represented no participation permitted; 1 represented participation with certain restrictions; 2 represented participation with no restrictions. A total score was then derived for each judge. The possible range was from 0 to 16. However, the maximum scored by any judge was 9.

[b]The scores included in each of the categories are: Much—7 to 9; Some—4 to 6; Very little—1 to 3; None—0.

ing active in various community and business affairs. As we have indicated, some judges feel very constrained, but others see nothing wrong in doing what other citizens are able to do. The following responses illustrate the judges' disagreement as to whether they should be allowed to participate in business affairs:

No! Without question! What if a judge owned apartment houses? How could he help but be influenced by it? We have no activities. That's why judges are poor. You pay a price for being a judge. We try desperately to observe this. We stay out of everything.

There's nothing wrong with that or being a millionaire. I have stock in banks and I'm not going to give that up.

Business affairs are especially controversial for judges because of the possibility of conflicts between private interests and public, judicial responsibility. This problem is solved in part by judges who excuse themselves from deciding cases in which they have a personal interest. However, this does not solve a different problem perceived by many judges—that a man's own values and preferences, which result from his private activities, will influence his decisions in cases which affect interests similar to his own. It is feared that in these cases a judge will identify with the litigant's cause. While all governmental officials face these problems to some extent, conflicts of interest are especially difficult for judges because popular and legal expectations call for judicial conduct to be completely free from any extraneous influence. As one judge put it:

He should definitely withdraw from business activities. I know of a judge who had some business holdings he couldn't dispose of. There was a dispute with another man and there was the possibility of litigation. Now how would that look? It's a matter of appearances again.

Demands that judges remove themselves from business and other off-the-bench activities are not simply abstract legal ideals or empty slogans. These expectations can be politically significant in a number of ways. First, they affect judges' perceptions of their role and suggest that judges differ in their off-the-bench conduct. Many judges stated, for example, that they had been active in a variety of organizations prior to recruitment to the court, but had resigned once they became judges in order to avoid improper appearances. In addition, as we have seen with regard to the Illinois case, judges who blatantly violate norms for judicial conduct may be removed or forced to resign from office.

Judicial ethics may also become a durable political issue which will be debated in a state for many years. A case in point is the character of judicial politics in Louisiana. As Table 4-4 shows, the Louisiana Supreme Court judges generally were more permissive toward judicial participation in off-the-bench activities. One issue which has been important in Louisiana for a number of years is the practice of many Louisiana judges (perhaps as many as fifty, according to a former dean of a Louisiana law school) of serving on the boards of directors of various local banks. One of the Louisiana Supreme Court judges reported that the chief justice himself had held one of these positions, but resigned from the bank when it became a major political issue.

Claims of bias and collusion stemming from judges' business contacts and activities have also been made in judicial election campaigns in Louisiana. For example, organized labor in Louisiana once charged that Chief Justice Fournet of the Louisiana Supreme Court led a majority of the judges in making an important decision favorable to a new oil drilling company on which Fournet served as a member of the board of directors.[11] In addition, it claimed that the Chief Justice and another member of the court majority had accepted Cadillacs from the president of the oil drilling company. The issue in the election campaign centered about the attempt by Fournet and the oil company to secure the election of a new judge to replace a recently deceased member of the favorable majority. Organized labor contended that the oil company was making large contributions to one of the candidates, and that the company had persuaded various political organizations in the New Orleans area to endorse the candidate it favored. Such events clearly indicate that judicial ethics and objectivity in decision making are more than vague judicial ideals; they may become crucial issues in state politics and may fundamentally affect the position and behavior of courts in the state policy-making process.

Conclusion

Viewing the courts through the concept of role focuses our attention on the relationships between judges and other actors in the political system, and highlights important aspects of judicial behavior involved in decision making. We are able to view courts as major political institutions which interact in various ways with other participants in state politics. Our discussion on the judicial role also has emphasized the need to view judges' orientations to their role in relation to personal, political, and judicial systems variables which affect their behavior. Judges' personal backgrounds and numerous features of the environment surrounding the courts affect the specific content of role orientations.

It has not been possible to investigate all features of the judicial role in this chapter; however, we have presented certain data on the work of state supreme court judges which illustrate some of the fundamental features of the appellate judicial role and some of the ways in which judges' orientations are affected by the state political environment. As expressed by judges themselves, the functions and objectives of appellate courts are varied and include performance of routine tasks and formal adjudication as well as opportunities to make law and to supervise the actions of the lower courts. The appellate judicial role also differs from the role of trial judges. Not only do procedures used for reaching decisions vary tremen-

11 *The Federationist,* 1958 (local labor news sheet).

dously, but certain supreme court judges also recognized the greater potential of the supreme court to make important policy through its decisions. This chapter has also touched upon the significance of judicial ethics as a political issue and the ways this aspect of the judicial role varies among the states.

V JUDICIAL
DECISION MAKING

Judicial decision making involves the process of transforming inputs through the judicial process into policy. Although we generally assume that judicial decisions involve actions by judges and juries in trials, the judicial process, in its broadest sense, includes many different actions by various officials throughout the administration of justice. The mass of issues that are settled before and without trial, the smaller number that come before judges and juries and the very few that are appealled are all politically significant. Patterns of decision making differ at each stage of the judicial process, but significant numbers and types of conflicts are settled at each level.

Only about ten per cent of all criminal cases come to trial and, although the evidence is not so clear and consistent, a similarly small proportion of civil cases ever get to court. Most criminal cases are settled through negotiated guilty pleas and civil cases often are settled out of court for sums of money and conditions agreed upon by both parties. The content of these decisions and the way they are made are important because they affect classes of litigants differently and they determine the quality and character of justice which is dispensed in the judiciary.

Trial and appellate court decisions occur less frequently, but because they are more formal and visible they more frequently provide opportunities for major judicial policy pronouncements. The great mass of trial court decisions provide opportunities for the courts to make collective contributions to judicial policy, but an opinion from a state supreme court may create the occasion for a much more visible and even innovative judicial policy pronouncement.

Because each stage of decision making is important in its own way, we will consider each level separately. Through individual consideration and comparison we can describe judicial decision making more completely.

In contrast to judicial decisions made in the courtroom, pretrial determination may best be described as processes of negotiation and bargaining which often lead to settlements without trial.[1] Pretrial settlements differ from courtroom decision making because they are informal, largely invisible to public inspection, and, particularly in criminal matters, closely linked to the political and social system. Morever, nothing in the pretrial process is automatic or predetermined; each stage includes alternative actions that may be taken by participants who have considerable flexibility and great discretion at each step.[2] This discretion means that each stage of the pretrial process may serve as an arena for final settlement of an issue, or may send it forward toward courtroom action. The flexibility and informality of pretrial actions make for a wide range of interactions and relationships among legal officials, attorneys, and litigants, in contrast to the constraints and formalities of the courtroom.

A factor encouraging bargaining and negotiated settlement is the presence of certain political and personal considerations in pretrial processes. For example, prosecuting attorneys concerned with advancing their political careers often prefer negotiated guilty pleas to boost their conviction rate, rather than take a chance on the outcome with a judge and jury in a trial. Defense attorneys and attorneys in civil cases also may prefer pretrial settlements which speed up the entire process, giving them time to take on additional legal work. Speed is a concern to judges, too, since most city courts are clogged with cases awaiting trial. Therefore, judges may encourage pretrial settlements to reduce the backlog of litigation.[3]

Decision making in trials takes place in the court room, is presided over by a judge, and is controlled by legal formalities. Although attorneys and public officials participate in trials, the decisions are made by juries or by judges hearing the case. Consequently, judicial decision making is more visible, more constrained by legal formalities, and more controlled in behavior than pretrial settlements.

Appellate decisions, made in all state courts of last resort, and in intermediate appellate courts of those states having such courts, differ in major respects from trial outcomes. Appellate judges become involved following trials when the loser may ask for review of the decision. Except in rare instances, appellate courts hear only appeals. Appellate court judges review

---

1 Actions in pretrial stages of the judicial process are described in Herbert Jacob, *Justice in America,* 2d ed. (Boston: Little, Brown and Company, 1972), Chap. 9.
2 For a study of guilty plea bargaining, see Jerome Skolnick, "Guilty Plea Bargaining: Compromises by Prosecutors to Secure Guilty Pleas," *University of Pennsylvania Law Review,* 112 (1964), 865–85.
3 Jacob, *Justice in America,* Chap. 9.

trial records and hear arguments by attorneys, but do not repeat the trial. Because state appellate courts have from three to nine members, appellate decisions depend upon agreement among the judges, and may also involve the expression of disagreements through dissenting opinions. In contrast to trials, appellate decisions are group judgments in response to the original trial decision rather than original decisions by a single judge or jury.

In this chapter we shall consider decision making in trial and appellate courts, and also examine certain features of pretrial settlements. However, existing research and information on judicial decision making is not distributed evenly, but is heavily weighted toward state appellate courts. Appellate decisions are published and collected systematically in state and regional law reporters. Trial court decisions, on the other hand, are rarely published, and no complete collection of decisions is readily available. Of course, they can be investigated by examining the files of local courts, but the great mass of decisions makes this very difficult. Consequently, much research on state court decision making focuses on appellate courts, and so our discussion will also emphasize this body of information.

RESOLUTION BEFORE TRIAL

Many important steps must be taken before the trial in criminal cases: an arrest must be made, a charge filed, the possibility of bail considered, prosecution decided upon, and a plea made. Only then can the trial begin. In civil cases equally important steps are necessary before trial is begun: the suit must be filed, the defendant must respond to the claim, and one party must refuse an out-of-court settlement that would compromise and resolve their differences. Thus, in both criminal and civil cases the process is complex and several steps must be followed before actual trial occurs.

In criminal prosecution the police have an important task in making the initial decision to arrest. Although police judgment must be hasty and usually on the spot, patterns of arrest decisions emerge, for various kinds of criminal conduct frequently are approached quite differently by the police. Some offenders may be arrested and soon released, as in the case of drunkenness, street brawling, and prostitution, while others, such as dope addicts, may be arrested and then referred to social agencies for treatment. Other types of disturbances, such as those stemming from family fights or bickering among neighbors, may be mediated by the police rather than considered causes for arrest. In contrast, persons committing serious crimes involving property and physical violence are regarded as subjects for prompt arrest.[4]

The discretion of the prosecutor in deciding whether to press charges after arrest has been made and in negotiating settlement of cases without trial has long been accepted as necessary and proper. The enormous authority of

[4] President's Commission on Law Enforcement and Administration of Justice, *Task Force Report: The Courts* (Washington, D.C.: U.S. Government Printing Office), p. 5; for a more detailed study of the functions of police, see Jerome Skolnick, *Justice Without Trial* (New York: John Wiley & Sons, Inc., 1966).

the prosecutor before trial has led some to speak of him as a "de facto judge." Much of the political sensitivity of the prosecutor's role is linked to the crucial character of his office, especially to the necessity for his maintaining a good record. This is ordinarily defined as a good record of case convictions, but may also include sensitivity to the social and personal problems involved in criminal prosecution. He is usually elected, often in partisan elections, and may use his office and the public record of his activities not only to keep his position but as a stepping stone to higher political office as well.[5]

The prosecutor may decide after an arrest has been made that there is insufficient evidence for prosecution, an important witness may refuse to cooperate, or new evidence indicating innocence of the arrested defendant may appear. The tactics of prosecution may sometimes lead him to drop less serious cases in exchange for the defendant's cooperation in giving testimony against a more serious offender, or he may decide to pass over minor offenses in order to save time and energy for the prosecution of really serious crimes. In some localities there is a precharge conference between the prosecutor and the defense attorney to discuss the possibilities of noncriminal disposition of the case, and perhaps to negotiate for dropping some or all charges in exchange for the defendant's cooperation in other cases.[6]

An important part of the negotiations among prosecutor, defendants, defense attorneys, and sometimes judges carries over into trials, particularly in the form of the negotiated plea of guilty. Indeed, the question of guilt or innocence is not contested in the great majority of criminal cases. Most guilty pleas are the product of negotiations between prosecutor and defense attorney and are intended to exchange the plea for a reduced charge or a favorable sentence recommendation by the prosecutor. Although there is much of this kind of explicit "plea bargaining," defendants also may plead guilty simply with the expectation, based on prevailing custom, that those who plead guilty and ease the job of prosecutor and judge will be sentenced more leniently.[7] The prevalence of negotiated guilty pleas in the trials of some states is indicated by Table 5-1.

While there is some variation among the states on the proportion of guilty pleas in trial courts, it is a high percentage of total convictions in all states. On the face of it, the practice appears advantageous for both prosecutor and defendant. It keeps the judicial system moving because it deals expeditiously with a large volume of cases, and it provides defendants

---

[5] See Herbert Jacob, "Judicial Insulation: Elections, Direct Participation and Public Attention to the Courts in Wisconsin," *Wisconsin Law Review* (Summer 1966), 801; Kan Ori, "The Politicized Nature of the County Prosecutor's Office, Fact or Fancy? The Case in Indiana," *Notre Dame Lawyer*, 40 (April 1965), 322–25.
[6] A discussion of recent trends may be found in President's Commission, *Task Force Report: The Courts*, pp. 9–13.
[7] President's Commission, *Task Force Report: The Courts*, pp. 9–13. The Supreme Court recently decided that plea-bargaining, as such, did not violate the constitutional principles of due process of law. Thus a defendant who decides voluntarily and on the advice of counsel to plead guilty and forego a trial may not claim, ex post facto, that he has been denied due process of law. *De Cavalcante v US* 30 L.Ed. 2d 731.

TABLE 5-1   PREVALENCE OF GUILTY
              PLEAS IN TRIAL COURTS OF
              GENERAL JURiSDICTION OF
              SELECTED STATES

State (1964 unless otherwise noted)	Total convictions	% Guilty pleas
California (1965)	30,840	74.0
Connecticut	1,596	93.9
Hawaii	393	91.5
Illinois	5,591	85.2
Kansas	3,025	90.2
Massachussetts (1963)	7,790	85.2
Minnesota (1965)	1,567	91.7
New York	17,249	95.5
Pennsylvania (1960)	25,632	66.8
Average		86.0

Source: *President's Commission on Law Enforcement and Administration of Justice,* Task Force Report: The Courts *(Washington,
D.C.: U.S. Government Printing Office, 1967), p. 9.*

with a bargaining point. It also has the important political effect of improving the prosecution record of convictions and making law enforcement look
efficient. Private attorneys who participate in bargaining are rewarded with
continued access to prosecutors and judges. Despite those apparent advantages, the basically informal and invisible manner in which the system
operates has led to criticism of the practice of the "negotiated guilty plea."
There is no element of due process in the system, and the defendant is
convicted without formal procedures or checks guaranteeing constitutional
protections. According to one critical survey of the practice, "The judge, the
public, and sometimes the defendant himself cannot know for certain who
got what from whom in exchange for what."[8] There is no judicial review
of the propriety of the bargain, and not only does the process take place
clandestinely, but in the sentencing stage there is often a pretense that no
bargaining took place in order to reach the guilty plea.

Equally invisible and informal are the other decisions reached in pretrial
criminal dispositions. In such decisions as arrest and charge bargaining
there is potential for coercion and undue pressures as well as for equity and
leniency. Unlike a formal trial, the informality of the process leaves out
the opportunities for checking and careful supervision that form so
important a part of the idea of due process.

Civil cases do not raise due process questions, and the character of
pretrial negotiation is somewhat different from that in the criminal process.
Most civil cases involve a period of informal negotiation during which the
lawyers try to reach a compromise settlement, usually involving a sum of
money. However, in some instances pretrial conferences are conducted more
formally. Many state judges, for example, require that the parties appear

[8] President's Commission, *Task Force Report: The Courts,* p. 9.

before them prior to their scheduling the case for trial. Even if a settlement is not reached, the attorneys can agree on the ground rules to be followed and perhaps stipulate certain issues that need not be covered at the trial. Thus, cases that do reach the trial stage can proceed more smoothly and quickly.

TRIAL BY SINGLE JUDGE OR BY JURY

Of those cases tried in courts, many are heard by single judges, while others go before juries. It is sometimes possible for defendants to choose whether to have their case tried by a judge or by a jury; therefore, there is considerable variation in the utilization of juries according to the kinds of issues involved and the region of the country. For example, plaintiffs in insurance and consumers' rights cases often prefer jury trials because they believe juries will be more sympathetic and generous to those claiming an injury; defendant insurance companies and corporations try to avoid juries. Apparently, use of juries is also dependent upon local custom. For example, the State of Georgia, with 144 jury trials per 1000 population, makes most frequent use of juries, while Minnesota and Connecticut, with three jury trials per 1000 population, use juries least often. Other state figures fall between these extremes, but generally the southeastern states use juries most frequently while northern states use them the least.[9]

The jury is particularly significant as the most important democratic input into judicial decision making. The legislature has its representative bodies, and the courts have their bodies of "twelve peers" to mitigate elite influences and provide channels for popular pressures in decision making. Participation of juries in making judicial decisions raises important questions concerning their behavior. What special values result from jury participation in deciding cases? Do juries consistently favor consumers and the injured over companies? Asked in another way, do juries come to decisions that are less fair and responsible and more populistic than the decisions judges would make in the same cases? These are important questions, because some legal experts have suggested that juries are an outmoded appendage of legal tradition, while others defend their value in democratic terms.[10]

There have been no systematic studies of jury decision making, but we have scattered examinations of jury functions and one major empirical study, Kalven and Zeisel's *The American Jury.* A major finding on which these studies agree is that judges and juries would come to the same decision in at least 75 percent of all criminal cases. The one out of four cases on which judge and jury disagree was the subject for extended analysis in *The American Jury,* the conclusion being that in one-half of these cases the

[9] Harry Kalven, Jr. and Hans Zeisel, *The American Jury* (Boston: Little, Brown and Company, 1966), pp. 502–3.
[10] Ibid. For a critical evaluation of *The American Jury,* see Michael H. Walsh, "The American Jury: A Reassessment," *Yale Law Journal,* 79 (1969), 142–58.

jury was giving rein to personal sympathies under the guise of factual investigation and analysis. This conclusion can lead to conflicting evaluations of the jury as decision maker:

To some, no doubt, the fact that judge and jury agree some 75 per cent of the time will be read as a reassuring sign of the competence and stability of the jury system; to others the fact that they disagree 25 per cent of the time will be viewed as a disturbing sign of the anarchy and eccentricity of the jury.[11]

Most of our knowledge of judges' decisional behavior concerns judges acting on appellate courts. Because of its dependence on group interactions, such information is not applicable to single judges. When a judge comes to a trial court he sheds his previous associations and does not have the opportunity of forming alliances with fellow judges. The trial judge thus lacks the potential that appellate judges have for associating in decision making with other judges of similar partisan or ideological persuasion. The formation of subgroups, such as a liberal faction, a civil rights bloc, or a conservative group, is also not possible for trial judges. This does not mean, however, that the trial judge comes into court tabula rasa.[12] Quite the contrary, the backgrounds of state judges reflect the socioeconomic character of the community and the locus of power within it. If a single party or faction dominates the community, it will also control judicial selection. Such associations are to be expected, considering the close fashion in which judicial recruitment is linked to state politics.

However, as in the analysis of appellate decisions, we can compare trial judges' decisions and seek to explain similarities and differences. Because the trial judge must decide for either the plaintiff or defendant in such common categories of cases as civil liberties, zoning, taxation, or consumer's rights, we can determine a voting record by noting the direction of votes. Although legal studies often seem to deny that trial judges consistently differ in making decisions, scattered political science studies indicate that there is as much consistent variation among trial judges' voting behavior as among appellate judges. In an analysis of trial judges in New York, Dolbeare found that: 1) there was considerable variation among judges voting in cases dealing with important policy matters, and 2) differences were consistent over time. Moreover, the lawyers who had to appear before trial judges were well aware of judges' decisional tendencies, and tried to arrange to appear before judges whose leanings best served their purposes.[13]

Explaining the differences and similarities among trial judges' decisional behavior poses some problems. One basic difficulty is lack of a sufficient number of cases upon which to base investigations. While all judges on an appellate court hear each case, each trial judge hears a separate case, thus

11 Kalven and Zeisel, *The American Jury,* p. 57.
12 On backgrounds of trial judges, see Wallace S. Sayre and Herbert Kaufman, *Governing New York City* (New York: Russell Sage Foundation, 1960), pp. 531–36, and Kenneth M. Dolbeare, *Trial Courts in Urban Politics* (New York: John Wiley & Sons, Inc., 1967). pp. 28–32.
13 Dolbeare, *Trial Courts in Urban Politics,* Chap. 5.

making it difficult to accumulate a large number of case votes in given categories. It also appears that trial judges do not always respond to the same factors that influence the decisions of appellate judges. For example, studies have shown that party affiliations affect behavior on the state appellate courts, where Democratic and Republican judges respond differently to certain kinds of social and economic policy cases. Dolbeare, however, did not discover differences among trial judges of different parties in New York. He also found that such differences in the judges' social background as religion and ethnicity did not correlate with their choices in decision making.[14]

Our limited evidence shows that trial judges' behavior is not as closely related to their personal characteristics as is appellate judges'. This may be due in part to their isolation from the political system and from other judges with similar backgrounds and ideologies. As a result, the trial judge has an opportunity to achieve more of the judicial ideal of "independence and detachment" in his decision-making role as solitary judge. Detachment means, in this instance, not only independence from outside pressures, but also from colleagues on the court. Trial judges' isolation permits them to pursue behavioral roles that are an idiosyncratic combination of attitudes toward public policy and the legal process. Thus, although trial judges may not differ in expected ways according to political and social features of their background, they may differ in their attitudes toward: 1) adherence to precedent and the exercise of reasonable discretion, 2) how much reliance should be placed on administrative agency or law enforcement actions, 3) what would be the practical effect on the government, society, or the courts of deciding the given case a certain way, and 4) preference for objectives of private enterprise or some other group aim.[15]

APPELLATE DECISION MAKING

Because data is more readily available for decisions made by appellate courts, their activities can be investigated systematically and their decision making processes described in some detail. In this section we emphasize three aspects of appellate courts. We begin by looking at the presence of conflict in decision making and levels of dissent. Second, we examine judges' individual policy preferences and consider explanations for differences in voting. Then we consider the processes involved in group interaction in judicial decision making at the appellate level.

Conflict in decision making

A basic problem in appellate courts involves securing agreement among the judges. Since state appellate courts have plural judiciaries, cases are decided by majority vote. Such courts always have an odd number of judges (three, five, seven, or nine) to discourage even divisions and tie

---

[14] Dolbeare, *Trial Courts in Urban Politics,* pp. 77–78.
[15] Ibid., p. 69.

votes. Voting on court decisions is even more formal than in legislatures, for the votes of judges generally are recorded and decisions are not made by voice votes. Moreover, the presence of conflict is more noticeable because judges who disagree with the majority may write a dissenting opinion which explains and justifies the basis for their disagreement. Records of agreement and dissent are important features of appellate decisions, for they reveal the extent and patterns of conflict on the courts.

Although conflict can be expressed in other ways, as in arguments in conference or in personal statements and memoranda to other justices, expression by means of a recorded dissenting vote has special importance. Votes of dissent are formal actions that apear in the record and emphasize disagreement. A decision delivered with dissents has political implications that are lacking in the unanimous decision, which conveys the appearance of total agreement. Moreover, courts with a great deal of dissent in their decisions operate in an atmosphere different from courts that are relatively free of dissent. Specifically, a court that habitually makes decisions on the basis of divided votes adjudicates in an environment of factions and personal difference. Rivalries and disagreement sometimes become public and tensions hamper interpersonal cooperation and agreement in arriving at decisions. Also, conflicts expressed in dissents may build, because dissents express animosities which reinforce conflict; interpersonal agreement is limited even further and more dissent is likely. A court that produces few split-vote decisions, on the other hand, operates in an environment of apparent harmony and agreement. The public facade of agreement creates a court lacking in open tensions and overtly expressed hostility. Such an atmosphere must surely help in reaching agreements and compromising differences; in turn, fewer dissents are produced and a harmonious environment remains.[16]

A good example of a contentious supreme court that regularly produces many divided decisions and vigorous dissents is the court of Pennsylvania. The contemporary Pennsylvania court is well known for the personal animosities, some of them public, among its members.[17] There are many other supreme courts that present public facades of harmony, among them the supreme court of Wisconsin. There are few records of dissension in the activities of the Wisconsin court, and personal animosity is rare. There exists an atmosphere of nonpartisanship and confidence in the ability of the court to resolve differences and effect compromises.[18]

Are state supreme courts more like the Pennsylvania court or the Wisconsin court? To provide material for comparison we have collected data on dissenting opinions for the supreme courts of 48 states (Hawaii and Alaska are omitted due to their relatively recent status as states). The data include figures for three years for each state, spaced over 25-year intervals. We have dissent rates for the years 1966, 1941, and 1916, which permits us to compare them over time.

Table 5-2 presents the rate of dissent in the state supreme courts for

16 Henry Robert Glick, *Supreme Courts in State Politics* (New York: Basic Books, Inc., 1971), Chap. 5.
17 Ibid., pp. 92–93.
18 David W. Adamany, "The Party Variable in Judges' Voting: Conceptual Notes and a Case Study," *American Political Science Review*, 64 (1962), 92–110.

TABLE 5-2   PERCENTAGE DISSENTING OPINIONS
IN STATE SUPREME COURTS
FOR THE YEARS 1916, 1941, AND 1966[a]

Rank in 1966	State	1966	1941	1916
	High Dissent Courts—Pennsylvania Model (Dissent rate > 20%)			
1	Michigan	46.5	19.0	9.6
2	Pennsylvania	41.0	5.0	1.5
3	New York	41.0	15.8	34.1
4	Ohio	34.9	14.1	14.8
5	California	32.3	16.7	5.3
6	Florida	28.2	17.7	4.1
7	Oklahoma	26.5	19.7	0.1
8	South Dakota	24.3	12.0	18.6
	Low Dissent Courts—Wisconsin Model (Dissent rate < 20%)			
48	Massachusetts	1.2	0.6	0.0
47	Alabama	1.7	4.1	6.1
46	Rhode Island	1.4	5.4	6.5
45	North Carolina	2.4	17.8	13.2
44	Tennessee	3.0	2.3	1.6
43	South Carolina	3.4	8.3	17.0
42	Delaware	3.4	15.4	15.0
41	Connecticut	3.6	3.9	11.9
40	Mississippi	3.9	8.0	0.1
39	Missouri	4.1	0.7	17.4
38	Maine	4.2	7.0	2.5
37	Vermont	5.9	1.7	5.4
36	Maryland	5.4	8.6	5.6
35	New Mexico	6.0	10.3	6.2
34	Arizona	6.1	1.8	8.3
33	Minnesota	6.8	10.8	5.9
32	New Jersey	7.1	30.2	14.0
31	Illinois	7.2	15.7	15.0
30	New Hampshire	7.3	1.4	3.3
29	Virginia	7.4	19.6	0.1
28	Wisconsin	8.0	3.9	8.6
27	Kentucky	8.1	3.0	0.1
26	Georgia	8.3	7.2	5.8
25	North Dakota	8.4	15.1	10.0
24	Idaho	9.0	35.6	12.2
23	Oregon	9.1	12.2	9.1
22	Wyoming	9.7	4.3	2.6
21	Nevada	9.8	6.8	11.4
20	Colorado	9.8	26.3	18.5
19	West Virginia	10.7	14.3	4.8
18	Nebraska	11.2	7.1	36.5
17	Washington	11.5	28.7	10.0
16	Indiana	11.5	5.7	7.1
15	Utah	11.7	33.0	7.7
14	Montana	11.9	16.1	0.1
13	Kansas	12.1	13.4	8.5
12	Louisiana	12.7	0.9	12.8
11	Arkansas	13.6	14.3	9.6
10	Texas	19.1	3.4	5.7
9	Iowa	19.7	14.4	5.2

[a]Includes per curiam but not memorandum opinions.
Source: West's state and regional reporters for 1966, 1941, and 1916.

the three different years. We note that dissent rates varied widely among the states in each period. In the most recent year examined (1966), dissent for the Michigan, New York, and Pennsylvania courts approached the level of the national supreme court (over 50 per cent) while dissents in Massachusetts, Rhode Island, and Alabama were barely more than 1 per cent of all decisions made. The figures for 25 years earlier (1941) and 50 years earlier (1916) also show contrasts among the states, but in many instances the states changed their level of dissent. That is, courts that ranked high in dissent in 1966 did not rank high in 1916 and 1941. A good example is Pennsylvania, whose 41 per cent dissent rate was not equaled in 1941 or 1916, when the rates' were 5 per cent and 1.5 per cent, respectively. On the other hand, some states which had rather high percentages of dissent in earlier years did not remain high by 1966. For example, Nebraska's court made 36.5 per cent of its decisions with dissents in 1916, but the percentage of dissents was only 7.1 per cent in 1941 and 11.2 per cent in 1966; Idaho had 35.6 per cent dissents in 1941 but 12.2 per cent in 1916 and 9.0 per cent in 1966.

The relationship among dissent rates in the three years is described in Table 5-3. These overall relationships confirm our impression that courts differ in the extent of conflict and agreement among judges during different years of their history. The low correlations indicate that change and development occur in dissent rates. For most states the changes do not follow an orderly pattern of increase or diminution. In addition, the average level of dissent remained much the same in state supreme courts over the 50 years covered in the tables. Although dissent has greatly increased in some courts, such as Pennsylvania's, in the states as a whole dissent rates have increased only 2 per cent since 1916. Unlike the national supreme court, which has developed into a factional court on which decision making is highly divisive, judges on state courts as a whole dissent relatively little. The picture of the average court, in 1966 as well as in 1916, is closer to the Wisconsin than to the Pennsylvania model. Most cases are decided without expressions of overt conflict in voting, and a facade of nonpartisan agreement and legal consensus is presented to the outside world.

One explanation which is helpful in accounting for variations in dissent among the states emphasizes social and political conditions that lead to division, conflict, and competition in politics. For example, differences in

TABLE 5-3   RELATIONSHIP OF
DISSENT RATES IN
STATE SUPREME COURTS
FOR THE YEARS 1966,
1941, AND 1916
(Pearsonian Product Moment
Correlation)

	1966	1941	1916
1966	—	.22	.15
1941	.22	—	.18
1916	.15	.18	—

interparty competition have been explained by variations in urbanism, industrial development, and character of a state's population. Perhaps certain social and economic conditions also lead to conflict and competition in judicial institutions. Possibly judges, who often have practical political experience before recruitment to the courts, bring with them attitudes and predispositions to interpret judicial policies in ways that reflect these basic social and political conflicts. In addition to partisan attitudes, judges might be motivated by issues reflecting urban-rural problems, civil rights, and economic attitudes. Any of these might surface in decisions which involve some aspect of the social and political conflict of a state.

We can investigate this hypothesis by observing whether judicial conflict embodied in dissents is associated with certain of these major social and political variables. If it is true, then judicial dissents should be higher in states with major internal social, economic, and political differences.

According to Table 5-4, several of the variables examined are associated with dissent rates in the states. They offer a suggestion as to why some state courts have more dissent than others in decision making. For example, there is some relationship between the urban and population makeup of the states and the tendency to dissent. Some suggestive relationships are also found in certain characteristics of the courts themselves. First, there is some indication that a tendency to dissent is associated with the number of judges on the court; that is, a greater number of judges increases the

TABLE 5-4   **RELATIONSHIPS BETWEEN RATES OF DISSENT IN STATE SUPREME COURTS AND CERTAIN SOCIAL AND POLITICAL VARIABLES (1966 Dissent Rates)**

| | Correlation with rate of dissent | |
Variable	All states	States with intermediate appellate courts
Background Variables		
Per cent urban population, 1960	.28	.40
Per cent foreign born, 1960	.16	.49
Per cent negro population, 1960	.12	.30
Multiple *R* of three variables above	.29	.51
Interparty competition (Ranney index)	.16	.33
Court Organization Indicators		
Number of judges on court	.35	.43
Total number of cases heard	.08	.23
Per cent of court dominated by one party	.31	.38
Per cent of total cases affirmed	.27	.34
Indicators of Other Government Programs		
Per capita state taxes, 1964	.02	.14
Number of state government employees, 1964	.28	.16
Public assistance expenditure, 1964	.12	.09

Source: The Book of the States, 1970–71; *Ranney, "Parties in State Politics"; and same as Table 5–2.*

likelihood of dissent. Second, dissent is related to the presence of inter-mediate appellate courts. The relevance of intermediate appellate courts for rates of dissent on supreme courts is that intermediate appellate courts, because of their special jurisdiction, decide many of the routine cases which are appealed, leaving more of the controversial and significant questions for the supreme court. Faced with a larger proportion of issues which concern major policies, judges on the high state courts are more likely to disagree on the outcome of the litigation, thus leading to higher levels of dissent.[19]

Table 5-4 shows that dissent rates of supreme courts in states with intermediate appellate judiciaries are related more strongly to such social and political factors as interparty competition, urbanism, and percentage of foreign born in the population. These social and political factors indicate heterogeneous populations and social and political conflict, which are in turn reflected in higher rates of dissention in the courts of these states.

The politics of judicial recruitment suggests an explanation for the link between judicial decision making and the political environment. Judges are usually political party actives with a background of political experience that ties them to the issues and conflicts of their particular states. The political past may be recalled when litigation presents issues and positions which the judge associates with his own political values. Thus, party actives who disagreed as participants in state politics prior to becoming judges may carry on this conflict after their elevation to the supreme court.

Political differences in judges' voting

Besides the impact of the political environment on decision making, dissent on state courts also means that there are personal policy differences among the judges. Although each case is argued on its legal basis, litigation also involves such political or social issues as civil rights, labor questions, rights of criminals, and divorce. Research on appellate decisions has shown that where there is disagreement on a court, judges often take consistent policy positions. A well-documented instance of political divisions among judges is the Michigan Supreme Court, where there have been durable factions on workmen's compensation and other labor-management cases.

Several studies have systematically investigated judges' voting on state appellate courts in an effort to explain patterns and differences in decision making. Generally, these investigations have related differences in judicial voting behavior to political party affiliations and personal background characteristics such as religous and ethnic affiliation. One examination of judges' voting was made by Stuart Nagel,[20] who investigated differences between Democratic and Republican judges in deciding cases, checking

19 Working independently, Bradley Canon and Dean Jaros have reached similar conclusions in "External Variables, Institutional Structure, and Dissent on State Supreme Courts," *Polity,* 3 (Winter, 1970), 175–201; on state intermediate appellate courts, see American Judicature Society, *Intermediate Appellate Courts,* Report no. 20 (Chicago: American Judicature Society, 1968).
20 Stuart Nagel, "Political Party Affiliation and Judges' Decisions," *American Political Science Review,* 55 (1961), 843–60.

particularly to see whether judges' votes corresponded with predicted Democratic and Republican positions on certain issues. Based on party ideology and tradition, he hypothesized that Republicans and Democrats would take the following positions on important policy issues commonly handled in supreme courts:[21]

1. In civil rights cases Democrats would support the claimant.

2. In taxation cases Democrats would support the claims of the government or taxing authority.

3. In workmen's compensation cases Democrats would support claims of workingmen.

4. In business regulation cases Democrats would support the claims of government as regulator.

5. In insurance cases Democrats would support the claimants against insurance companies.

6. In criminal cases Democrats would vote for the defense.

7. In labor-management cases Democrates would vote for the labor unions.

8. In debtor-creditor cases Democrats would vote for the debtor.

9. In landlord-tenant cases Democrats would vote for the tenant.

10. In employee injury cases Democrats would vote for the employee.

On all these issues Republicans would support the opposing side.

In a comparative analysis of state courts Nagel gathered data on the votes of all appellate judges in the 48 states for cases decided in 1955. The votes were then compared to the political party affiliations and to the ethnic and religious background of the judges. All three features of judges' background—partisan affiliation and ethnic and religious characteristics— were found to be related to votes on the cases. Moreover, in all the categories listed above. Democratic and Republican judges decided in the predicted way, although some relationships were stronger and more significant than others.[22] Nagel's work contained no analysis to indicate which of the three judicial background characteristics was most important for judicial behavior. The relative importance of background variables is a vital question, for there is considerable overlapping among the traits. For example, various ethnic and religious groups have been influential in the development of Democratic party membership, and these same groups would be represented in the state judges. That is, individual judges who might be Democratic or Republican in party affiliation would also have certain ethnic and religious backgrounds. We cannot be sure without further analysis which feature of the judge's social and political background shapes his judicial behavior.

Nagel's study raised so many questions that a number of persons have replicated his research, or at least portions of it. One replication which followed Nagel closely was Bowen's study of appellate judges' decision making. Using somewhat more careful statistical methods, but also departing from some of Nagel's research design, Bowen confirmed the observation

21 Nagel, "Political Party Affiliation and Judges' Decisions," p. 844.
22 Ibid.

that groups of judges with similar background characteristics tended to vote differently from judges with other characteristics. After his careful analysis he concluded that "a number of these associations hold up with astonishing consistency over a large number of different types of cases."[23]

These intriguing findings concerning judicial behavior, particularly the impact of party affiliation upon judges' decisions, have also been investigated for a number of individual states. In Michigan, party affiliation has been shown to be strongly related to patterns of decision making on the supreme court. Michigan judges, although nominally elected in a nonpartisan system, are previously nominated by party conventions. Consequently, their partisan identity, rather than being hidden, is strongly emphasized in Michigan politics. During his lengthy tenure as governor of Michigan, G. Mennen Williams undertook to "pack" the supreme court by securing the election of a majority of members who were "Williams Democrats." When he took office Williams governed in company with a supreme court dominated by a Republican majority of 6–2.

There were no vacancies on the court during his first five years of office and Williams and the court disagreed frequently on certain social and economic policies. During the next two years, however, five vacancies occurred on the Michigan court to be filled at regular and special elections. Due to his increased influence within his party Williams was able to secure the election of judges amenable to his own policy outlook in all five positions. Thus, Governor Williams was eventually able to govern with a supreme court which favored his policies more frequently. The result was a major reorientation in the voting line-up of the justices. The new liberal majority consisted of four Williams Democrats and one non-Williams Democrat with the Republican justices in opposition and dissent.[24]

Another investigation of four state supreme courts with high dissent rates (New York, Pennsylvania, California, and Michigan) showed that background characteristics were inconsistently related to variations in judges' decisions. In Pennsylvania, Michigan, and California, partisan identifications of judges were found to be associated with different decisional tendencies, while in New York little relationship was discovered. In Pennsylvania and Michigan the partisan association was strong; in California it was only moderate.[25]

A cogent demonstration that divisions in case votes are sometimes not due to partisan affilations may be found in David Adamany's investigation of the Wisconsin court.[26] Such division as has occurred in the court's dissenting behavior is unrelated to the party divisions of the justices, due to the genuine nonpartisan environment in which the Wisconsin court operates.

23 Don Ramsey Bowen, "The Explanation of Judicial Voting Behavior from Sociological Characteristics of Judges" (Ph.D. dissertation, Yale University, 1965), p. 57.
24 Sidney Ulmer, "The Political Party Variable in the Michigan Supreme Court," *Journal of Public Law*, 11 (1962), 352–62; Glendon Schubert, *Quantitative Analysis of Judicial Behavior* (New York: The Free Press, 1959), pp. 129–31.
25 Malcolm McCollum Feeley, "A Comparative Analysis of State Supreme Court Behavior" (Ph.D. dissertation, University of Minnesota, 1969).
26 Adamany, "The Party Variable in Judges' Voting," pp. 92–110.

Unlike Michigan, where nonpartisanship was only nominal, the entire election process of Wisconsin judges from nomination through balloting has been marked by an absence of activities along party lines. Indeed, if anything, judicial elections in Wisconsin are bipartisan in character. Judges are nominated in nonpartisan primaries, and in campaigns receive support from both parties and from legal and news media elites who join in a bipartisan effort. Moreover, even the electorate votes along bipartisan lines, and balloting in judicial elections is not strongly associated with partisan patterns in other elections.

As we have indicated, there seem to exist two models of decision making in state supreme courts. One, exemplified by the Michigan and Pennsylvania courts, occurs in a milieu of factionalism expressed in dissenting opinions. Often the character of differences in voting behavior is associated with such significant background factors as ethnic-religious affilation, age, state, religion, and political party. Of these, the strongest involvement is with political parties; partisan division may actually help produce factions on the courts which lead to dissent. The decisional differences often continue outside of court and are expressed in judges' rivalry in party affairs and other political contests. The second type of court, exemplified by Wisconsin, usually has a low dissent rate. Such consistent divisions and opinions as can be found are only weakly associated with social and political features of the justices. The court presents an effective facade of nonpartisan, legal consensus in which differences are resolved by informal procedures and implicit agreements. Disagreements are not openly expressed either in decisions emanating from the court or in activities outside the court. At present the typical state court of last resort appears to be more like the Wisconsin than the Michigan-Pennsylvania model.

Group interaction in decision making

Many of the supreme courts with low dissent rates are located in states with considerable political conflict and diversity. This conflict may be observed in issues brought before the court and in the selection of judges, whose backgrounds reflect political differences. The political and social differences in some of these states are as sharp and as visible as in those states where supreme courts have high dissent rates. Wisconsin, for example, has a low dissent rate and a nonpartisan facade in decision making; yet the state of Wisconsin has as much party competition, and as many diverse interests and sharp political disagreements as do the state environments of Michigan and Pennsylvania. Judges on the Wisconsin court also reflect as many political and social differences in their background as do the Michigan and Pennsylvania judges.

Finding courts with varying dissent rates in states with similar political environments indicates that there are other important differences in the way the judges handle disagreement and conflict. In the Pennsylvania and Michigan Supreme Courts, personal differences and disagreements operate throughout decision making and are recorded as votes in numerous split decisions; in Wisconsin and other similar states, while disagreements occur in the process of reaching decisions, they are settled prior to or without a formal vote, and an image of agreement and harmony is presented.

Reaching agreement on an issue often involves various personal interactions among the judges. Although specific procedures differ, several common methods by which courts handle decision making provide the judges with various occasions to interact. Following the close of oral arguments and presentation of briefs, judges hold a conference during which each presents his views of the case and the decision he favors. The chief justice presides over this conference, in which the justices speak in a prescribed order. In some states the most senior judges speak first, while others, following the lead of the United States Supreme Court, have the junior judges speak first. After a discussion an informal consensus may exist or an initial vote may be taken to determine whether one view of the case has a majority. If a majority exists, the chief justice will assign one member of it to write the majority opinion. This opinion is then presented to the court, and will be officially recorded if a majority continues to support it. However, if the opinion does not receive support the case will be reassigned and opinions revised until a majority is reached. Any concurrences and dissents to the majority decision will then be recorded, with the possibility that one or more members of the dissenting group will be chosen by that group to write a dissenting opinion representing their view.[27]

Discussions which occur in conference, numerous telephone calls and memoranda between judges, and informal conversations all provide opportunities for judges to air their differences and work out disagreements. Our interviews with state supreme court judges and other research reveals that there are four ways in which state courts handle the expression of disagreement and work to achieve a decision:[28] 1) persuasion, 2) compromise, 3) logrolling, and 4) voting. Of the four methods, the first three enable the judges to present a facade of legal certainty and bipartisan unanimity to the outside world. The fourth, settling the differences only by voting and recording the different opinions, presents a court that appears dissentious and divided.

Persuasion is utilized when, after differences become evident, judges urge other members of the court to accept their views by arguing with vigor and eloquence or through skillful analysis of the case. Because of the different amounts of influence exercised by the chief justice or by other judges with special status because of seniority or personal esteem, certain members of the court may be "persuaded" to abandon their own positions. Thus, differences may be settled when the views of one judge or a subgroup win over other members of the court.

To settle differences through processes of mutual give and take rather than by argument or persuasion is what is meant by *compromise*. A judge agreeing to include or remove a section of his opinion in order to gain the

27 Glick, *Supreme Courts in State Politics*, pp. 110–11.
28 Glick, *Supreme Courts in State Politics*, and Robert J. Sickels, "The Illusion of Judicial Consensus: Zoning Decisions on the Maryland Court of Appeals," *American Political Science Review*, 59 (1965), 100–104.

support of other judges is an example of such compromising of his own point of view to achieve consensus.

Another method of reaching agreement by exchanging support, similar to the exchange of support in the legislature, has been termed *logrolling*.[29] This way of securing unanimity has been described at work in the Maryland Court of Appeals, where the method by which support is traded to avoid dissent and conflict is to follow the lead of the opinion writer. Because opinions are rotated among members of the court, the practice has developed of allowing the opinion writer in certain cases to determine the direction of the decision; other members of the court then go along with him, and he in turn follows them when they write opinions. This results in some internal policy contradictions on the court, but the facade of unanimity is preserved and written dissents are largely avoided.

When persuasion and compromise fail to resolve conflicts, or when logrolling is not used, cases finally must be settled by formal *voting* which often results in published dissents. A dissent can be recorded simply as a disagreement with the majority opinion, or it can be accompanied by a written dissenting opinion. As discussed above, the publishing of dissenting votes and written opinions is an important aspect of decision making because dissents officially question the validity of the majority opinion. Although formal voting often results in recorded dissents, there are instances when it may not. For example, a judge dissenting by himself or with only one other colleague may not insist that the opposition be listed with the majority opinion. They may feel that their dissent has no effect on the impact of the majority decision or on the legal rules the court has established, and therefore prefer to have it noted only by the other judges on the court.

Of the four methods for reaching decisions, formal voting and its accompanying dissents reveal the level of political conflict that can occur on state courts and the differences which emerge over court decisions. Of course, many court cases are routine, but others evoke opposition and disagreement among judges which are linked to major political and social divisions in state politics, and are made visible by judges committed to their own interpretation of law and preferred public policies. Dissenting opinions question the validity of the majority vote and imply through their publication that they deserve equal billing with the majority opinion. Moreover, a widely held view is that if dissents are published they may one day supplant the majority opinion when similar issues are raised in court and a new set of judges is hearing the case.[30]

The presence of frequent dissents, as in Pennsylvania, represents more than simple disagreement among the judges, for disagreements can always be settled by discussion or argument (persuasion), interpersonal negotiation (compromise), or exchange of support (logrolling). Frequent dissents indicate major areas of disagreement that cannot be settled by means other than formal voting. Disagreements that are voted are public displays of an

---

[29] Sickels, "The Illusion of Judicial Concensus," pp. 100–104.

[30] See, for example, Michael A. Musmano, "Dissenting Opinions," *Dickinson Law Review*, 60 (1965–66), 152–53; Stanley H. Fuld, "The Voices of Dissent," *Columbia Law Review*, 62 (1962), 926–29.

institutional schism, and suggest that the court is an institution incapable of reconciliation or compromise, and that nonpartisan solution of problems is impossible.

Confronted by these implications, some judges of highly dissenting courts have defended dissents by recourse to both legal and democratic theory.[31] They argue that expression of differences is institutionally healthy, that policy differences ought to. be openly argued and debated, and that they have a democratic right to express their point of view. Moreover, they argue that such expression of differences assists the development of law by establishing a decisional dialectic. Judges on Wisconsin-type courts, on the other hand, argue for reconciliation of differences before voting. They stress the importance of a nonpartisan legal variety of decision making in which differences are subordinated to more important legal and institutional values.

The chief justice has special potential for influencing decisions in judicial decision making. His personal position, as well as his seniority and official status on the court and any skills he possesses in legal analysis and persuasion, afford him an opportunity for influence in court deliberation. However, some chief justices do not possess eminence and are hardly more personally influential than any other justices. But all chief justices possess the power of decision management through formal leadership on the court. Decision management results from the power of the chief justice to assign the writing of opinions, his presiding powers over the conference, and his direction of the consideration of cases. Also important are his functions in setting the timing and flow of the consideration of decisions. Although his influence doubtless varies among the states, some state judges consider his role in judicial decision making to be particularly important, and there is some evidence that, where the chief justice is active and respected in decision making, the amount of formal voting is reduced and dissenting opinions are minimized.[32]

31 Glick, *Supreme Courts in State Politics,* pp. 95–100.
32 Ibid., pp. 114–17.

VI JUDICIAL POLICY MAKING

Court decisions do more than settle disputes between litigants. Of course, they are important to those directly involved in specific cases, but court decisions also help to determine the social and political values which predominate in a political system, they frequently affect the distribution of substantial sums of money, and they can even determine political relationships among governmental officials and political parties. Although the processes involved in judicial policy making differ from legislative and executive action, courts are important policy making institutions, and we must view their decisions as integral parts of the political process.

CHARACTERISTICS OF JUDICIAL POLICY MAKING

A fundamental characteristic of judicial policy making is that courts cannot make policy until a case is presented to them for decision.[1] Unlike a legislature, which can initiate action and pass laws designed to implement its policies, courts must wait until others become involved in a conflict and bring it into court

[1] The following discussion relies in part on Richard S. Wells and Joel B. Grossman, "The Concept of Judicial Policy-Making," *Journal of Public Law*, 15 (1966), 296–307, and Herbert Jacob, *Justice in America* (Boston: Little, Brown and Company, 1965), Chap. 3.

for settlement. If cases concerning a particular issue are not brought before the judges, they cannot make policy. Occasionally a court will invite additional litigation through statements in opinions which suggest that the judges will make a decision which settles basic issues if certain new or more fundamental conflicts are brought before the court. In this way a court can increase its policy-making potential, but it still is dependent upon lawyers and litigants to initiate a case and shape the issues presented for decision.

Judicial policy making is also different because courts may not appropriate money or levy taxes to carry out programs. This is an important restriction on judicial policy making, for the ability to spend money to carry out programs is a crucial function of state and national governments. Almost all major policies in the states, including education, transportation, and welfare, depend on expenditures of great sums. The major actors involved in these policy areas are the governor, legislators, various interest groups, and political parties. Courts sometimes make decisions which regulate the operation of governmental programs (such as decisions concerning state qualifications of welfare recipients), but they are not involved in important decisions concerning allocation of money, consideration of policy alternatives, and development of specific programs.

Judicial policy making is not as programmatic as policies made elsewhere. Legislatures and administrative agencies can adopt policy goals and create extensive programs designed to accomplish specific purposes. A highway program, for example, includes plans for roads throughout the state, the manner and responsibility of financing and maintenance, and specifications for construction, letting bids, and so on. In contrast, courts are limited to making decisions in individual cases. They sometimes seek to develop policies which have an impact beyond the current example, but this cannot compare with the highly detailed, comprehensive programs produced by other state agencies.

The distinctive character of judicial decision making also affects formulation of judicial policies and the way information relevant to decisions is gathered by the courts. Judicial decision making is dominated by the adversary process in which judges are presented with fairly rigid alternatives by opposing sides in a case. The decision reached by the court almost always reflects support for one of the two alternatives, thus limiting the range of judicial policies emanating from individual court cases.

Judicial policies are additionally restricted because the information contained in the briefs and oral arguments of attorneys are neither unbiased nor necessarily complete, since they are designed to persuade the court to make a decision favoring a particular interest. Judges do their own research, but this is generally limited to the search for pertinent precedents, statutes, or legal theories. Besides the legal aspects of the case, there are social and economic relationships which will be affected by the decision of the court, but the judges do not have extensive access to information relating to these. Since decision making is supposed to exclude all but the judges themselves, the judges are insulated from possibly useful information not found in law books or in their own areas of expertise. Judges sometimes consult privately with experts outside of court, but this is not usually considered a legitimate part of the legal process. Since it must occur surreptitiously, most judges probably would not consider using outside sources in the process of coming to a decision. This aspect of judicial decision making contrasts sharply with the legislative process, in which public and private hearings are held to obtain relevant information and different points of view and legislators depend a great deal on the expertise of interest groups to provide them with information pertaining to a particular statute.

The form in which judicial policies appear and are communicated also makes judicial policy making different from legislative or executive action. Judicial policies are found most frequently in court decisions and written opinions. Decisions indicate the solution adopted by the court to deal with the conflict presented in the case, and opinions explain and justify the decision. In almost all instances, opinions are stated in legal terms and the basis of the decision is said to rest on judicial precedents, interpretations of statutes or constitutions, legal texts, and similar sources. Since these special terms use ideas and symbols not usually present in the actions of other governmental agencies, court opinions often do not make the policy content of a decision explicit. Despite these restrictions, court decisions do allocate resources and contribute to the ideas and values of society. Many times actions (policies) are of equal or greater significance than those of other governmental officials.

SOURCES OF JUDICIAL POLICIES

As we have indicated, judicial policy making differs from policy making in other political institutions, but there are several important variations in the ways judicial policies are made. The most frequent way is through court cases, from which policies can be produced in two basic ways: they can result from the decision in a single major case, or they can develop gradually as a pattern of action emerges from the decisions in a series of cases dealing with a similar problem. Certain cases, for example, involve major political or economic problems, such as reapportionment of a state legislature, the constitutionality of a new state tax, or the judicial definition of obscene literature. The issues in these cases are clear, they are important to many people not directly involved in the case, and they are usually expected to have a major impact on the behavior, values, and resources of a state or community.

However, many other cases do not have these characteristics. Thousands of traffic cases, minor criminal cases, and cases in small claims courts are handled by various state and local courts each year. The decisions in these are important primarily to the litigants themselves because their personal interests are at stake; the general public is not affected and very few people give much attention to this large body of litigation. These decisions may be significant, however, if they contribute as a group to the gradual evolution or development of a court policy. For example, the decisions of a court in a group of zoning cases may constitute a policy if the court tends to solve certain problems in a similar way, or if it tends to grant the demands of certain litigants over those of others. Each individual decision is not significant, but when they are combined and considered as a set or series of decisions they may contribute to the formation of a zoning policy.

Opportunities for making policy in a single decision usually are much greater in appellate than in trial courts. The characteristics of the courts give appellate judges certain advantages in the policy-making process. An important feature of appellate courts is that the decisions are usually accompanied by written opinions in which the judges express their reasons and can indicate the significance or impact that the decision is intended to have. These decisions may become precedents to be followed by all state courts in future decision making. Trial judges, on the other hand, are not usually expected to be policy makers. Conceptions of the judicial role frequently distinguish between the significant policy-making powers of appellate courts and the more limited conflict-settling duties of trial judges. Appellate judges have broader powers and jurisdiction than trial judges, they generally deal with more important issues, and they are less restricted by the status quo and local interests.[2]

Although decisions in court cases are the most visible and frequent sources of judicial policy, judges may seek to extend their policy-making authority by attempting to influence decisions made by legislators and executive personnel. Their efforts may be intended to achieve several objectives: establish a policy which cannot be made by the courts because of limitations on the scope of judicial power; to alter existing statutes in order to increase the future flexibility of judges in making decisions, and to pass new laws which will enhance the breadth of the court's current decisions.[3]

A survey of state supreme court chief justices reveals that the most frequent way in which supreme courts attempt to influence policy is through their comments in written opinions.[4] Judges may thus suggest the need for legislative action in policy areas dealt with in specific court cases. Occasionally, supreme court judges send copies of their opinions to legislative leaders, hoping to draw legislative attention to the issues raised. In addition, over half of the supreme courts hold conferences with legislators and about one-quarter of the courts have contacts with governors or other executive personnel. These direct contacts are considered very useful in focusing the attention of other officials on questions of policy deemed important by the supreme court.

Policies on which state supreme courts seek action by other officials most frequently concern the state judiciary itself, and touch on problems of court administration, organization, judicial salaries, regulation of law practice,

2 Kenneth M. Dolbeare, *Trial Courts in Urban Politics* (New York: John Wiley & Sons, Inc., 1967), pp. 124–25.
3 Most information about the ways judges seek to influence legislative and executive policy in order to achieve their own policy goals is found in research on the U.S. Supreme Court. See Walter F. Murphy, *Elements of Judicial Strategy* (Chicago: University of Chicago Press, 1954), pp. 123–55.
4 The following is taken from Henry Robert Glick, "Policy-Making and State Supreme Courts: The Judiciary as an Interest Group," *Law and Society Review*, 5 (November 1970), 270–91.

and court procedures. However, other important policy recommendations are made in such areas as criminal law, workmen's compensation, property and mortgages, and taxation. One chief justice reported that the state supreme court had been consulted by the legislature concerning whether a new court, an administrative agency, or the existing court structure should be used to deal with a new policy problem involving conflicts over the ownership of certain property. As we have discussed earlier, changes in court structure and the addition of judges frequently become major issues which affect the interests of political parties and other groups having a stake in litigation and resulting judicial policies.

In their efforts to influence legislative and executive policy, state supreme courts sometimes work with state judicial councils, which are organizations created by the legislature designed to study the operation of the state judiciary, court rules and procedures, and related matters in order to make recommendations concerning necessary changes in judicial structures. About half of the states have judicial councils that actively function as advisory agencies. Frequently the judicial councils make recommendations on their own or in conjunction with those of the supreme court. Besides judicial councils, trial court judges and bar associations may also try to influence legislative and executive decisions. There are instances when these groups cooperate with state supreme courts and act as allies in the policy-making process. However, they are also potential competitors when their interests conflict with those of the supreme court.

TYPES OF JUDICIAL POLICIES

Innovative policies

Innovative decisions in judicial policy making involve major issues not considered previously by the courts, or indicate a fundamental change in the judicial policy of a particular state. Innovation is not generally expected in judicial policy making because it is contrary to the value placed on precedent and judicial and legal traditions for dealing with recurrent problems. Innovative decisions receive the greatest amount of news coverage and public attention because they frequently concern controversial issues and are clearly intended to affect the decisions of other courts and other governmental officials, and to make extensive alterations in social, economic, or political conditions. They may require a reordering of fundamental values in the community and may produce opposition to court efforts to change the status quo. These kinds of decisions can be found in a variety of subject areas, such as civil rights, legislative reapportionment, rights of criminal defendants, prayer in the public schools, and retention of the death penalty.

The significance of innovation in policy making is reflected in the decisions produced by state supreme court judges included in the four state role study. The New Jersey Supreme Court, it will be recalled, was composed almost entirely of lawmakers and pragmatists, whereas the Louisiana judges were strongly oriented to the law-interpreter position. The decisions of these two courts varied considerably: the New Jersey court produced numerous decisions clearly aimed at producing new policies, while the Louisiana judges were reluctant to accept changes in the law. In one year the New Jersey judges produced innovative decisions concerning liability and damages in auto accidents, favored extension of legislation requiring the state to compensate lawyers who represented indigent defendants, extended certain constitutional guarantees to juveniles in criminal cases, considered changes in the imposition of the death penalty, and produced several important changes in trial procedure. The Louisiana judges tended to interpret statutes in a restrictive fashion, resisted changes affecting time-honored precedents, and opposed the expansion of judicial and other governmental power. A case in point in Louisiana concerned a claim for personal injuries in which the majority opinion writer stated that the court could not expand the meaning of existing statutes because both the state and federal constitutions prohibited the courts from exercising a lawmaker role. Moreover, since the legislature had not acted to clarify the terms of the statute in question, the court would not extend the interpretation previously attributed to the law.[5]

Some additional indication of the importance of the state courts in making innovative decisions can be found in reports contained in *State Government News,* a monthly periodical published by the Council of State Governments. This publication reports the major decisions of state agencies and institutions. The court cases it includes involve only a small portion of all the cases decided by state courts, limited to those considered sufficiently important to be reported, along with the decisions of legislatures and governors, as major state governmental decisions. These cases clearly indicate, however, that courts have an important impact on state policy making, and that they sometimes are highly innovative.

Almost all of the cases included in the *News* emanate from state supreme courts, for only rarely do trial courts make decisions deemed as important as those handed down by appellate courts. Occasionally, however, trial courts do become involved in controversial issues. In Utah, a trial court upheld the constitutionality of a state statute giving the legislature the power to appoint members of the state board of higher education. The governor had challenged the statute which limited his political power.[6] Although such cases appear occasionally, the policy-making role of the trial courts is limited largely to the more subtle and gradual development of policies through a series of decisions.

In order to illustrate the areas in which state supreme courts produce innovative policies, we have arranged decisions made by state supreme courts over a five-year period according to subject, and have listed the number of supreme courts which made innovative decisions in each category (Table 6-1). Some of these cases, such as those dealing with the rights of criminal defendants, civil rights, and legislative reapportionment, are familiar because they have been controversial issues in American politics for many years. The rights of defendants have received the greatest amount

5 Henry Robert Glick, *Supreme Courts in State Politics* (New York: Basic Books, Inc., Publishers, 1971), Chap. 2.
6 *State Government News,* 12 (September 1969), 3.

TABLE 6-1   **INNOVATIVE POLICIES IN STATE SUPREME COURTS, 1964–1969[a]**

Constitutional rights of defendants and criminals   (N = 16)
Civil rights   (N = 7)
Taxation   (N = 7)
Governmental regulation of business   (N = 5)
Elections   (N = 5)
Legislative apportionment   (N = 4)
Other suits against government   (N = 8)

[a]Our use of the concept of policy innovation follows that of Walker. See Jack L. Walker, "The Diffusion of Innovations Among the American States," *American Political Science Review,* 63, 1969, 880–89.
Source: State Government News, *7–12 (1964–1969).*

of attention, and several state courts have made more than one major decision in this area.

In addition to these more visible cases, state supreme courts have also made important decisions in taxation, elections, and governmental regulation of business. The significance of these cases as sources of major state policy is sometimes very great. The New York and Massachusetts Supreme Courts, for example, made decisions in 1968 which are directly opposed to the landmark decision of *McCulloch v. Maryland* (1819) in which the United States Supreme Court decided that national banks are exempt from taxation by state governments. These dramatic departures from previous court policies were contrary to legal opinions which had been published by many state attorney generals in recent years. These decisions, which have implications for all national banks in the United States, involve large sums of money. The bank in the New York case, for example, had paid $31,000 in taxes to the state which it was unsuccessful in having returned.[7]

The importance of innovative decisions can also be seen in two election cases. The West Virginia and Idaho Supreme Courts recently ruled that provisions of their state constitutions which required more than a simple majority (50 percent plus 1) of affirmative votes to designate approval of bond issues violated the fourteenth amendment of the United States Constitution because the affirmative votes had less impact than the negative votes cast in these elections. The two supreme courts held that both bond issues, which had received a simple majority of affirmative votes, should be certified as having been passed.[8] These decisions have significant political implications because they make it much easier for funds to be provided for such public projects as school construction, roads, fire and police protection, and sewage plants.

In addition to these cases, the California Supreme Court recently made a highly innovative decision concerning the procedures and formulae used to finance the state's public school system.[9] As in most other states, California's method of school financing was based upon local property valuations and

[7] *State Government News,* 11 (January 1968), 4.
[8] *State Government News,* 13 (January 1970), 5.
[9] Serrano v. Priest, Sup., 96 Cal. Reporter 601 (1971).

taxes available in each school district with supplemental state funds provided to the poorer school districts to raise available money to a minimum base level. In this case, a group of parents contested that, despite such state efforts at equalization, substantial differences remained among school districts throughout the state. As a result, the quality of the schools depended upon where one lived and the wealth of the area. The lower courts ruled in favor of the state and upheld current policy, but the state supreme court accepted the claims of the parents and stated that the current funding procedures discriminated against the poor and therefore violated the equal protection clause of the Fourteenth Amendment. The court argued further that property assessments are an improper and irrelevent basis for school funding, thus questioning the method by which local governments throughout the United States raise money for schools as well as other local projects. By declaring current state policy unconstitutional, the supreme court required the creation of a new policy to provide genuine equal education throughout the state, but equally important the court cast new attention to fundamental and traditional methods of local government financing.

It must be added that not only do the supreme courts make innovative decisions in important issue areas, but certain courts make more innovative decisions than others. The California and New Jersey Supreme Courts, for example, each made six innovative decisions in the five-year period included in Table 6-1. The courts of New Mexico and Pennsylvania are next with four decisions each, and the Illinois, New Hampshire, and Utah Supreme Courts each made three innovative decisions. Although no clear patterns exist among the states, it seems that certain courts are more likely to make new policies than others.

Controversial policies without innovation

In addition to far-reaching innovative decisions, state supreme courts make other significant policies. These policies may not have direct implications for future cases and other litigants and they are not necessarily innovative, but they sometimes have a tremendous impact on current political controversies. Such a case occurred in 1965 when Governor George C. Wallace of Alabama sought to have the state legislature pass a law permitting him to run for reelection. Existing Alabama law prohibited a governor from running for reelection immediately after his first four-year term. Part of Governor Wallace's strategy to change the law involved ending a legislative filibuster against his election bill by having the state supreme court declare unconstitutional the senate's rule that a filibuster could be terminated only by a two-thirds vote of the members. However, declaring that the legislature was a separate and equal governmental institution with freedom to make rules governing its procedures, the supreme court refused to decide the issue in the governor's favor.[10] This decision was not a new policy, but it was significant in preventing Governor Wallace from continuing as the governor of Alabama.

Another case having an important impact on state politics occurred when

10 *The New York Times,* 14 October 1965, p. 40.

the Florida Supreme Court ordered Governor Claude Kirk to make available to a duly established legislative committee on elections the membership roles and other documents of the Governor's Club, a private organization with the ostensible function of raising money for the governor's reelection campaign. The club became an important political issue when several state legislators charged that, in return for their $500 membership fee, contributors received liquor licenses, state contracts, and political appointments. The alleged link between club membership and political favors provided Kirk's opponents with a powerful campaign issue. Had the supreme court ruled in Kirk's favor, permitting him to keep the details of the club secret, the governor would have had an advantage over his adversaries.[11]

Cumulative policies

Innovative and controversial decisions are the most visible types of judicial policies, but they constitute a small percentage of the total output of state courts. Most decisions are not significant by themselves as sources of policy; however, when considered with other, similar cases, they may contribute to the gradual evolution or progression of judicial policy. Although this kind of policy is more difficult to uncover and analyze, it too determines which demands will be satisfied or denied in the political process, and how particular problems will be managed. As our discussion will show, cumulative policy making is important both in state appellate and state trial courts.

In order to examine this form of judicial policy making, we have examined the decisions made by four state supreme courts in a single year. To begin our discussion, Table 6-2 lists the various categories of cases heard by the courts. State courts become involved in a large number of issue areas, but some types of cases clearly predominate. Appeals from criminals are the most prevalent, and it should also be noted that a substantial portion of these cases raise issues concerning the violation of constitutional rights by police, trial judges, or other public officials. (In Pennsylvania, almost all of these cases are phrased in terms of constitutional questions and generally involve writs of habeas corpus). Other cases described in Table 6-2 include various civil suits against some governmental official or agency. These include tax cases, suits concerning the taking of property for public use, and a variety of other cases, such as disputes over results of civil service examinations, the granting of building permits, and personal injuries suffered on public property. Cases concerning motor vehicle accidents, other kinds of personal injury, and disputes between governmental agencies or officials also contribute significantly to the work of state supreme courts.

The great variety of cases decided by state supreme courts is significant in two ways. First, the courts have opportunities to affect policy governing a large number of social, economic, and political relationships. (In many areas of policy, court decisions are the major sources of law.) Legislative acts and local ordinances are sometimes important, but in many instances the legislature or city government has not acted and the courts themselves determine policy. At other times legislative acts are too vague or general

11 *Tallahassee Democrat*, 25 February 1970, p. 1.

TABLE 6-2   TYPES OF CASES DECIDED BY FOUR
                   STATE SUPREME COURTS IN 1965–1966
                   (in per cents)ᵃ

Issue	N.J. (N = 140)	Mass. (N = 314)	Penna. (N = 379)	La. (N = 88)
Criminal	21.4%	7.6%	1.6%	29.5%
Constitutional question in criminal case	11.4	5.4	26.1	13.6
Government regulation of business	2.1	6.1	1.6	6.8
Other suits against state and local				
government	12.1	15.9	12.9	6.8
Divorce	0.0	3.2	0.3	3.4
Motor vehicle accident	6.4	3.2	11.6	4.5
Personal injuryᵇ	7.2	10.2	7.9	6.8
Intergovernmental dispute	9.3	2.5	1.1	1.1
Contract	1.4	6.1	2.9	1.1
Wills, trusts, and estates	0.0	3.5	7.9	0.0
Insurance coverage	1.4	1.9	1.3	5.7
Real estate	0.0	4.1	2.9	3.4
Disbarment or disciplining of attorney	5.0	0.0	0.5	3.4
Zoning	2.9	7.0	1.3	0.0
Otherᶜ	19.3	23.2	20.1	13.8
Total	99.9%	99.9%	100.0%	99.9%

ᵃSeveral cases in which the issues were not stated are excluded.
ᵇThis category contains cases other than those concerning motor vehicle accidents or personal injury suits against government.
ᶜThis category includes a wide variety of issues in which there were only one or a few cases. Included are cases involving freedom of speech, labor-management, creditor-debtor, sale of consumer products, elections, unemployment compensation, and landlord-tenant disputes.

to be applied easily to problems presented to the court. Under these conditions judges must apply the laws according to their own interpretations of the intent of the legislature.

The variety of state court decisions is also significant because it includes many issues generally not considered by the federal courts. Not only do courts in the 50 states make more decisions than the federal courts, but such categories as criminal cases, workmen's injury or unemployment compensation cases, motor vehicle accident cases, and personal injury and damage suits are not usually decided by the federal courts. Therefore, state courts make the final decision in the large majority of these cases, and as a result are especially important in their own realms of judicial policy making.

As our discussion has indicated, Table 6-2 shows that certain types of cases are generally important in all four state supreme courts. However, several differences among the four courts suggest that judicial policy making varies from state to state. One important difference exists in the number of cases decided by each court during the year. The New Jersey and Louisiana Supreme Courts heard many fewer cases than the courts in Pennsylvania and Massachusetts. One explanation for these variations can be found in the differences in the jurisdiction of the four courts and the extent to which writs of certiorari are used to create their workload. The jurisdiction of the New Jersey and Louisiana Supreme Courts has been limited to a smaller variety of cases than has the jurisdiction of the courts in Pennsylvania and Massachusetts. This means that the New Jersey and Louisiana Supreme Courts are obligated by statute or the state constitution to grant hearings only to selected types of cases, while the Pennsylvania and Massachusetts courts must hear many more cases. All four courts may also issue writs of certiorari, which are decisions granting a hearing to a case which the court is not required by law to decide.[12] However, since the Pennsylvania and Massachusetts courts are required to hear so many cases, the writ of certiorari is much less significant in determining their workload than it is in New Jersey and Louisiana.

Given the opportunity to use their own discretion in determining a large portion of their workload, the New Jersey and Louisiana Supreme Courts may select cases which they consider to be especially significant, whereas the Pennsylvania and Massachusetts Supreme Courts have little such choice. There may be many cases in these two states which are unimportant as sources of public policy and in which the proper legal solution is clear, but which nevertheless require a supreme court decision. For example, even though almost all criminal appeals in Pennsylvania raise an issue concerning denial of constitutional rights and request for a writ of habeas corpus, the overwhelming majority of these requests are summarily denied, without lengthy opinions and generally without dissent. Only about 5 per cent of all Pennsylvania cases involving constitutional questions include controversies which are given serious consideration by the supreme court. This is close to the percentage of cases involving constitutional questions in Massachusetts. However, in contrast, it is interesting that a large percentage of criminal cases in New Jersey and Louisiana raised significant constitutional questions. This would seem to reflect the smaller number of other types of cases decided by the courts and, in turn, their ability to devote more attention to what they consider significant.

Besides variations in the number and types of cases which courts decide, the extent to which courts favor one interest or demand over another provides additional information about the content of judicial policy. In Table 6-3 we present several categories of litigants who have become involved in court cases and the frequency with which they have won and lost cases before state supreme courts. There are several important variations in Table 6-3 which suggest that the kinds of interests affected by state court decisions vary, and that certain courts are more responsive to some demands than to others.

It is clear that numerous interests are present in court cases and, as discussed above, state courts play a substantial role in various fields of policy making. However, some interests are involved in court cases much more frequently than others. For example, various agencies of state government participate in numerous cases in all four states. A large portion of these cases concern appeals by convicted criminals, but this leaves many cases involving state government in other forms of litigation. Although less

12 For a summary of the jurisdiction of state courts, see the state pages in annual issue of the *Martindale-Hubbell Law Directory* (Summit, N.J.: Martindale-Hubbell, Inc.). See also annotated state statutes for each state.

TABLE 6-3 VICTORIES AND LOSSES OF LITIGANTS IN CASES ARGUED BEFORE FOUR STATE SUPREME COURTS (in per cents)[a]

Litigants[b]	N.J.			Mass.			Penna.			La.		
	W	L	N	W	L	N	W	L	N	W	L	N
State government	62.1%	37.9%	(66)	55.3%	44.7%	(103)	72.5%	27.5%	(131)	78.7%	21.3%	(47)
Local government	51.4	48.6	(35)	50.8	49.2	(63)	58.9	41.1	(56)	37.5	62.5	(8)
Criminals, prisoners	31.7	68.3	(41)	37.5	62.5	(40)	25.7	74.3	(105)	18.9	81.1	(37)
Lawyers	25.0	75.0	(12)	50.0	50.0	(4)	60.0	40.0	(5)	20.0	80.0	(5)
Businesses	38.5	61.5	(26)	47.5	52.5	(101)	40.1	50.9	(112)	50.0	50.0	(24)
Employers	28.6	71.4	(7)	40.0	60.0	(10)	70.0	30.0	(10)	0.0	100.0	(2)
Employees	70.0	30.0	(10)	45.9	54.1	(37)	23.8	76.2	(21)	100.0	0.0	(3)
Operator of motor vehicle	30.0	70.0	(10)	66.7	33.3	(9)	43.6	56.4	(32)	0.0	0.0	(0)
Injured persons	61.5	38.5	(13)	40.0	60.0	(25)	53.1	46.9	(64)	71.4	28.6	(7)
Property owners	33.3	66.7	(9)	54.9	45.1	(51)	48.7	51.3	(39)	40.0	60.0	(10)
Claimants of estate	57.1	66.7	(9)	50.0	50.0	(32)	50.0	50.0	(76)	40.0	60.0	(55)
Other individuals	61.9	38.1	(21)	48.2	51.8	(114)	42.3	57.7	(71)	45.0	55.0	(20)
Other groups	61.5	38.5	(13)	81.8	18.2	(11)	52.4	47.6	(21)	100.0	0.0	(3)

[a]Cases in which the identity of the litigants is unclear are excluded.
[b]The litigants are identified according to the major role they represented in court cases. For example, although owners of businesses are usually also employers, it their role in a court case concerned them as the owner of a business, and not as an employer, they are identified here as businesses.

frequently than state agencies, local governments also participate in a large amount of litigation. As stated, criminal appeals account for another large group of cases. Finally, it is important to note the significance of conflicts involving businesses of various sorts in the litigation of the courts. From the figures in Table 6-3, it would appear that state courts have numerous opportunities as well as obligations to influence the development of governmental policy concerning commercial relations as well as the role of administrative agencies in regulating business affairs.

Besides the variety of interests affected by supreme court decisions, it is significant for state court policy making that there are differences as well as similarities among the courts in terms of their reactions to different demands. All four courts tend to favor the demands of state government; however, as suggested above, many of these victories reflect unsuccessful appeals by criminals. Agencies of state government do less well in other cases, but still win between 50 and 68 per cent of their cases in litigation in the four states. In contrast to the level of success enjoyed by state government, criminals and prisoners in all four states lose many more cases than they win. Many criminal appeals are final efforts that do not raise issues of sufficient importance to lead appellate courts to overturn lower court decisions.

Table 6-3 suggests that there are also subject areas in which state court decisions differ. Using these four courts as examples, we see that the claims of businesses and employers receive less support from the New Jersey Supreme Court than they do elsewhere. (Louisiana had only two cases involving employers, but they lost both times.)

In contrast, employees involved in various cases do much better in New Jersey and Louisiana than they do in Massachusetts or Pennsylvania. Litigants suing for damages (personal injuries) have also won more frequently in New Jersey and Louisiana than in the other two states. However, it is interesting to note that the Louisiana Supreme Court is least receptive to the claims of criminals and prisoners.

These findings suggest that various policy orientations are adopted by the state courts, and that certain social and economic interests are more likely to be successful in litigation before them. For example, the New Jersey court in particular and the Louisiana court to some extent adopt a more liberal stance toward certain economic interests. The tendency of these courts to favor employees, to oppose employers and businesses, and to favor those who have been injured in various accidents contributes to a pattern of decision making which is responsive to liberal demand.[13] However, the Louisiana Supreme Court is more conservative in criminal cases.

Similar differences will probably be found in most state courts, for the types of interests involved in litigation and the demands which they make reflect similar social and economic positions. Certain interests will be more successful depending on the particular state, for the political environment of state politics and the backgrounds, experiences, and attitudes of judges

---

[13] It is interesting to note that interviews with the New Jersey judges indicated that several of them perceived a liberal majority to exist on the court.

are several factors which help to account for variations in judges' policy preferences and the direction of court decisions.

Our earlier discussion focused on differences in the policy-making roles of different state courts. We indicated that trial judges were less able to make significant policy decisions in a single case, but that their decisions in a series of similar cases may constitute the gradual development of a policy. It is primarily through such cumulative policy making that trial courts become major policy-making institutions.

An example of the significant policy-making role of trial courts is found in the decisions of a New York City criminal court. The fines imposed on landlords who violated the city building code had steadily decreased an average of 26 per cent from one year to the next. The imposition of fines for building violations had been part of an effort to curb the growth of slum housing in the city, but since the fines had dropped from an average of about $19 a case to $14, they were viewed simply as "another business expense" and ceased being an effective technique for enforcing the building codes.[14] These decisions are a small part of governmental policy making in a city the size of New York. However, slum housing, urban renewal, and racial strife are interrelated issues, and the courts are part of the governmental machinery which attempts to cope with them. These decisions of the courts, therefore, are significant aspects of a highly controversial area of urban policy making.

Kenneth M. Dolbeare has examined the policy-making role of trial courts by focusing on the content and direction of certain cases decided by the trial courts of a large New York county over a period of fifteen years. Dolbeare selected only those cases which involved decisions of other political officials and dealt with issues that were of general importance to the community. In part, Dolbeare was interested in determining the role played by the trial courts in supporting or altering the decisions of other public officials. Excluded were criminal cases, divorce cases, auto accident cases, contract disputes, and other similiar civil litigation which did not involve issues having direct and significant implications for the general public.

Dolbeare discovered several kinds of cases in which the trial courts had an opportunity to make decisions affecting county policy. Table 6-4 includes the number and kinds of these cases and the frequency which the courts supported the decisions made by others. The trial courts generally supported the decisions of officials in cases dealing with nominations and elections and public education, and so their impact in these policy areas was negligible. However, in tax cases the courts imposed property valuations very different from those set by county officials, and also declared certain new local taxes void. Dolbeare concludes that the trial courts had a substantial impact in this particular policy area. In cases dealing with licensing and other forms of business regulation, the trial courts tended to favor business interests, and carefully reviewed governmental procedures for regulating commercial relations. The courts also had a major influence on determina-

14 *The New York Times,* 19 August 1965, p. 33.

TABLE 6-4   **PUBLIC POLICIES AFFECTED BY
TRIAL COURTS AND THE SUPPORT
GIVEN TO OTHER GOVERNMENTAL
DECISIONS BY THE COURTS**

Policy area	Number of cases	Percentage support for other governmental decisions
Nominations and elections	16	75%
Education	25	80
Taxation	9	33
Licensing and other regulation of business	30	43
Government powers and procedures	34	62
Zoning and land use	190	51

Source: Derived from Kenneth M. Dolbeare, Trial Courts in Urban Politics *(New York: John Wiley & Sons, Inc., 1967), pp. 108–9.*

tion of governmental powers and procedures. However, the largest single group of cases raising important issues of public policy were in the areas of zoning and land use. The courts generally opposed the standards set by governmental officials when they interfered with the demands of business to use property for business purposes.[15]

Viewed within the broader context of policy making, Dolbeare concludes that the trial courts have a major effect on shaping the final content of public policy in certain issue areas, but that the policy-making role of the courts is limited.[16] Trial courts have all of the characteristics and limitations of judicial policy making discussed earlier. In particular, since courts do not initiate action, but must wait until a case has been brought to them, there are various policy areas generally unaffected by the courts. This does not mean that the courts are unimportant in policy making, but that judicial policy making in trial courts is significant only in certain issues.

RELATIONSHIP BETWEEN STATE AND NATIONAL JUDICIAL POLICY

We stated previously that state courts make decisions in many kinds of cases that are rarely dealt with by the federal courts. As a result, the state courts are the most significant policy-making institutions in particular areas of judicial policy. The significance of state court decisions is amplified even more when we consider the relationships which exist between state and national judicial decisions.

As the highest judicial authority in the nation, the United States Supreme Court makes numerous policy decisions which are intended to be national policies. They are supposed to be adopted by all state and federal courts when these courts confront cases similar to those that prompted the initial

---

[15] Dolbeare, *Trial Courts in Urban Politics,* pp. 106–11.
[16] Ibid., p. 111.

Supreme Court decision. For example, the U.S. Supreme Court has made important decisions in recent years in a variety of policy areas: rights of defendants in criminal cases, reapportionment of state legislatures, civil rights, prayers and Bible-reading in the public schools, and other questions which have had a fundamental impact on social and political values throughout the country. The significance of U.S. Supreme Court decisions lies not only in the fact that, as the highest court, it determines broad outlines of national policy, but also that state courts are obligated to follow the direction of national policy in their own decisions.

However, lower court judges throughout the United States do not always adopt the policies of the U.S. Supreme Court. This means that, in addition to their final authority in most cases which come before them, state judges also become key policy makers in cases in which a national standard has been created. There are various techniques for avoiding or circumventing national judicial policies. One of the most frequent is through the interpretation given to a U.S. Supreme Court decision and the way the state judge chooses to apply the decision to specific facts and issues before him. A decision by the U.S. Supreme Court is frequently ambiguous because it specifies only the broadest outlines of policy and does not indicate precisely how its rules are to be applied in other cases. State judges are thus accorded considerable discretion in applying these decisions to their own cases, and the results achieved can differ tremendously from what was intended.[17] This occurs even in cases in which the U.S. Supreme Court has reversed a state supreme court and returned the case to the state court for further proceedings, often on other, more specific issues. One study has shown that during a ten-year period, in a total of forty-six cases returned to state courts for further litigation, about half of the litigants who were successful before the U.S. Supreme Court *lost* the case when the state supreme court made its subsequent decision.[18]

State courts sometimes adopt procedures, rules, and other policies which prevent application of national judicial policy to state cases. The Florida Supreme Court, for example, has made it very difficult for prisoners to seek appellate review when they contend that their constitutional rights have been violated. The court has required strict adherence to proper forms and procedures for submitting petitions to the supreme court, even though most of the litigants are unfamiliar with legal terminology and procedures and do not have access to attorneys while in prison. Their petitions are frequently rejected because of incorrect preparation.[19]

This court has also interpreted national court decisions so narrowly that the policies are made inapplicable to most state cases. It has refused to extend decisions guaranteeing the right to counsel and the right to

---

17 Walter F. Murphy, "Lower Court Checks on Supreme Court Power," *American Political Science Review*, 53 (1959), 1018–31.
18 "Evasion of Supreme Court Mandates in Cases Remanded to State Courts Since 1941," *Harvard Law Review*, 67 (1954), 1251–59.
19 "Gideon, Escobedo, Miranda: Begrudging Acceptance of the United States Supreme Court's Mandates in Florida," *University of Florida Law Review*, 21 (Winter 1969), 346–58.

remain silent to certain stages of the judicial process which it has termed "extrajudicial" and therefore outside the regulation and control of the courts. As a result, statements and confessions made without the presence of an attorney and without the prisoner being warned that what he says may be used against him in court have been declared admissible as evidence in several cases. The court also has not made these constitutional rights applicable to convictions for misdemeanors.[20] Rejecting the applicability of a particular court policy to other similar cases is a tactic used by other courts as well. For example, suits that have relied on school desegregation decisions as a basis for seeking the desegregation of public transportation and other public facilities sometimes have been rejected by judges who would not permit school desegregation policy to be made applicable to desegregation of buses, city parks, and other public places.[21]

Because state judges have considerable discretion in interpreting U.S. Supreme Court decisions, the policies adopted in the states may follow or deviate from the pronouncements of the high court. In race relations cases, for example, Negroes generally have received more favorable treatment by state supreme courts in all but one of the peripheral southern states (North Carolina, Tennessee, Texas, and Virginia) than they have in the deep south states. In addition, the Supreme Courts of Tennessee, Texas, and North Carolina have openly acknowledged the authority of the decisions of the U.S. Supreme Court in race relations, and have declared state efforts to maintain segregation unconstitutional. However, deep south state supreme courts, maintaining a state's rights position, have clearly expressed their disagreement with national desegregation decisions and have sought ways to avoid compliance with national policy.[22] In these states it has been very difficult to make state judicial policy consistent with U.S. Supreme Court decisions, thus emphasizing the independent impact of state judicial policy.

---

20 Ibid., pp. 352–55.
21 Murphy, "Lower Court Checks on Supreme Court Power," p. 1028.
22 Kenneth N. Vines, "Southern State Supreme Courts and Race Relations," *Western Political Quarterly,* 18 (March 1965), 11–15.

INDEX

A

ABA (American Bar Association), 10, 11,
     15, 29
Adamany, David, 84
Adjudicator, judge as, 60, 61, 63, 64,
     68
Administration of courts, 92
Administrator, judge as, 60, 61, 68
Alabama, 80, 96
Alaska, 37, 78
American Bar Association (ABA), 10, 11,
     15, 29
American Judicature Society, 15
Amicus curiae briefs, 7–8
Appeals, 18, 28–32, 35
Appellate courts, (supreme courts),
     28–33, 35, 37, 70–71
   collegial, 56
   cumulative decisions by, 97–103
   intermediate, 28–31, 35, 37, 71, 82
   judges on, 56–59, 71–72, 76, 77
   judicial decision making in, 77–88
   judicial role in, 59–65
   policy-making opportunity of, 92
Appointment of judges, 39–41, 44, 47, 49
Appropriations for courts, 4
Arizona, 30
Auto accidents, 94

B

Background of judges, 83–85
Backlogs, 26–27
Banks, 95
Bargaining with prosecutor, 73, 74
Bowen, Don Ramsey, 83
Brennan, William J., 2
Briefs, 7–8
Business law, 23
Business litigation, 24
Business regulation cases, 83, 95

C

California, courts in, 11–13, 29, 30, 34,
     37, 40–41
   dissent rates in, 84
   innovative decisions by, 95–96
Charge bargaining, 73, 74
Chicago, 17, 25
Chief justices, 88
Civil cases, 74–75
   See also specific cases
Civil rights cases, 83, 93–94, 104, 105
Collegial appellate courts, 56
Colonial courts, 19–21
Competition, interparty, 82

About the authors

HENRY ROBERT GLICK, associate professor of government at Florida State University in Tallahassee, is the author of *Supreme Courts in State Politics* (1971) and co-editor of *Prisons, Protest, and Politics* with Burton Atkins (Prentice-Hall, 1972). His research on American state courts also has appeared in numerous professional journals.

KENNETH N. VINES is professor of political science at the State University of New York at Buffalo. He has been active in broadening research into all levels of American judicial behavior. In addition to articles in professional journals, Professor Vines has written *The Politics of Federal Courts* (with R. J. Richardson, 1970) and edited *Politics in the American States* (with H. Jacob, 1965, 1971).

PRENTICE-HALL FOUNDATIONS OF STATE AND LOCAL GOVERNMENT SERIES
WALLACE S. SAYRE, Editor

STATE LEGISLATIVE SYSTEMS
Wilder Crane, Jr. and *Meredith W. Watts, Jr.*
STATE COURT SYSTEMS
Henry Robert Glick and *Kenneth N. Vines*

By analyzing judicial institutions in a political science framework, STATE COURT SYSTEMS reevaluates the role of state courts in American democratic processes. Through careful research, the authors cut through the usual covertness of judicial activities and the lack of media coverage about judicial politics and present their findings of how state courts operate as a political system. This book offers a new view of the judiciary, analyzing the functions and powers of courts as value-allocators and representations of partisan politics, as well as lawmaking and policy-making institutions. Clarifying the problems in terms of systems analysis, the authors view the judiciary as a major political institution that interacts in various ways with other participants in state politics.

Prentice-Hall, Inc., Englewood Cliffs, New Jersey   0-13-842